D0129073

WEIGHING THE ODDS IN SPORTS BETTING

KING YAO

Pi Yee Press

WEIGHING THE ODDS IN SPORTS BETTING

by
King Yao
Pi Yee Press

ISBN 0-935926-30-5

Printed in the United States of America in 2010

 3 4 5 6 7 8 9 10

ABOUT THE
AUTHOR

King Yao is the author of *Weighing the Odds in Hold'em Poker*. He uses his experience from making millions in financial derivative markets and translates it into gambling. Since he left his trading position in 2000, he has been playing poker and betting on sports. He travels to Las Vegas frequently, especially during football season. He keeps a blog at http://weighingtheodds.blogspot.com and is a regular poster on Internet forums dedicated to sports bettors.

Contents

LIST OF TABLES

Table 24 Kentucky Derby Winners Below 10-1 175
Table 25 Kentucky Derby Winners Above 10-1 176
Table 26 Number of Entrants in Major Races 177
Table 27 Belmont Stakes Odds for TC Candidates 179

ACKNOWLEDG-MENTS

Thanks to all the people who helped me with this book. These people provided comments, suggestions, constructive criticism and helpful thoughts. This book is better due to their input. These people include Brett Rogers, Nick Christenson, "Joeflex," Derek Miller, Jesse Gregory, Don Peszynski, Elihu Feustel, Jeff Fogle, "NajdorDefense," Mike Sullivan, Michael Bodel, Jesse F. Knight, Dunbar, Jan Suchanek, Albie O'Hanian, Brian Dwyer, Chuck Wolff, and the great people at LTS.

Thanks to posters on Internet forums who have helped me directly and indirectly with ideas and thoughts on sports betting. There are too many to name them all; apologies to those I missed. In particular, I learned a lot from these posters via posts they made as well as direct emails and personal contacts: "StevieY" and "Colin Caster" from SharpSportsBetting.com, "Fezzik," "Cutter," "Hizzle," "Math Boy," "Lawboy," Trace Fields, George Abel.Fields, and Jeff Brueggman

Thanks to Jon Spevack, who posts as "Jon in Oakland" and organizes a weekly conference call for sports bettors that can be found at http://www.sportsconferencecall.com/.

Thanks to Howard Schwartz of the Gambler's Book Shop for his support and advice on the structure of the book.

Thanks to Ed Miller and Bryan Clark, the previous editor and the current editor of *Two Plus Two Internet Magazine*. Thanks to Mason Malmuth of Two Plus Two. The articles I wrote for the magazine gave me the idea to write this book. Many of those articles have been incorporated into this book.

Thanks to my former colleagues and bosses at Susquehanna Partners, especially Tom Peters, David Yuen, Jim Doughan and Jeff Yass. All of my experience in the financial markets came while trading for Susquehanna.

Thanks to Stanford Wong for publishing this book, my second book with Pi Yee Press. Thanks to Al Rogers of Pi Yee Press for making things run so smoothly.

Thanks to Joanne LaFord of JOW Graphics for creating the cover of this book. Her web site is jowgraphics.com

Thanks to my family who have always been incredibly supportive. This book is dedicated to my wife, Shirley Woo, and our son, Cameron.

The 2008 printing has minor corrections and clarifications; it has no material that is not in the 2007 version.

CHAPTER 1
INTRODUCTION

The Purpose of This Book

Sports betting can be attacked intelligently. Smart sports bettors do not gamble the same way as tourists play roulette or retirees play the slot machines. Instead, smart sports bettors are making bets that they have thought through carefully with supporting logic and/or research. The purpose of this book is to give you tools to succeed at sports betting, to show you how to evaluate, compare and view sports betting from an analytical perspective, not from a gambling perspective.

This book should be used as a guideline to sports betting rather than a blueprint. The sports betting market changes and adapts quickly. The underlying principles shown in this book should help you adapt and continue to make good bets even when the market changes.

This book is for you if you want to think analytically about sports betting. It is for you if you do not want to be spoon-fed supposed winners, but want to get some ideas to improve your game. You battle bookmakers and line makers constantly; betting sports is a game of maneuvers and adjustments. You can use as many weapons as possible in this continuous fight. This book should help in that regard.

Organization

Chapters 1 through 7 are on general theory and ideas in sports betting. These chapters should be read first as the rest of the book builds on their ideas. The remaining chapters can be read in any order. Chapters 8 through 17 examine more in-depth issues in particular sports. These chapters give you a sense of how to attack different aspects of sports betting using analytical tools, market perspectives and logical reasoning. Chapters 18 through 24 have information and general advice while covering multiple sports. At the end of the book is a glossary.

Other Books

There are few quality books on sports betting. The first sports-betting book that I recommend is *Sharp Sports Betting* by Stanford Wong. A few other sports-betting titles contain good information, including books by Don Peszynski, Kevin O'Neill, Trace Fields, Scott Kellen and Mike Murray. You also can get information from sports books that are not geared towards betting, and use that information to suit your purposes when it comes to handicapping and betting. Compared to other forms of gambling, there are relatively few good books on sports betting.

There are many knowledgeable sports bettors who have the ability to write quality books on their craft. Why have so few of them written books on the subject? Unfortunately, the financial reward they expect to get from writing a book is probably not worth the effort. Instead, writing a book may hurt a sports bettor's future winnings if disseminating his secrets decreases his future betting opportunities. You implementing the author's ideas means more competition to make the same bets as the author. Most bettors who have the knowledge to write quality sports-betting books decide it is negative EV (EV is explained in chapter 2) to give out information when the expected royalties from a book are relatively small compared to the size of their wagers. In addition, it takes time and energy to write a book. Instead of writing a book, skillful sports bettors may sell information in the form of picks, which will probably net them more income than royalties from a book. Selling picks does not require any explanations, so they do not have to reveal their methods.

Why I Wrote This Book

When I wrote my first book, *Weighing the Odds in Hold'em Poker*, I did not have to think about the possibility that I would cost myself money by giving out information. If you use some of the ideas I wrote about in my hold'em book, it is unlikely to affect me directly since there are so many poker players, so many hold'em tables and so many poker rooms.

Sports betting is different from poker in that it is a worldwide market similar to a financial market. If someone in New Zealand makes a large wager, it is possible that his wager can affect me directly by moving the line on the game around the world, thus denying me the opportunity to make the same wager at the same line. The sports-betting marketplace has similarities to the financial world. I was able to transfer my training and experience in trading options and other derivative products to sports betting. The information in this book is some of the things I have learned during that time.

I have analyzed and bet on sports for a long time, but it was after finishing writing *Weighing the Odds in Hold'em Poker* that I turned my main focus on sports betting. There are many different ways to approach sports betting, and the more I delved into it, the more interesting and challenging I found it. You can approach it from a handicapper's point of view and try to make a better line than the line makers and the market. Or you can approach it from a relative-value player's point of view and make distributional, correlated and derivative bets. Or you can approach it from the point of view of a scalper or middler. There are numerous ways to attack the sports betting market and find positive EV.

I did enjoy the process of writing *Weighing the Odds in Hold'em Poker* and decided to write about some of the things I learned about sports betting. In February, 2006, I submitted my first article to the *Two Plus Two Internet Magazine*, which can be found at TwoPlusTwo.com. That article, on the analysis of a Super Bowl prop, is the foundation for chapter 12 of this book. I enjoyed writing the article as it forced me to focus on a specific topic and explore it in-depth and from different angles. After a few months of writing articles, I started thinking about writing a book, the book that you now are reading.

I knew I had to make sound logical arguments if my writing were to be published. But I was also prepared for the possibility that someone might catch an error, which actually did happen with that first article. I did not mind being corrected since learning from my mistakes allowed me to improve both my writing and my own betting. The same logic applies to this book: If you find an error, please tell me about it. I am both a sports bettor and a writer, and willing to improve in both endeavors.

I wrote this book is to satisfy my own ego. There are few good books on sports betting, so my contribution to the literature will be more significant than a similar effort in another field. My enjoyment of the writing process and my ego outweigh the possible negative EV in writing the book, thus making it positive EU (expected utility) for me.

Why Sports Betting?

I enjoy following, betting, and thinking about sports more than I enjoy following stocks, thinking about interest rates and trading in the financial markets. I would rather analyze how Alex Rodriguez will perform in his next playoffs given his poor past performance than how PAC IOs will perform given an increase in mortgage refinancings. I would rather evaluate how often a baseball team is expected to win by more than 1 run given certain variables than evaluate the skewness of an out-of-the-money put in the Pharmaceutical Index. I would rather compare the relative strengths of the Colts and Patriots when playing on a cold November night in New England than compare the relative differences in volatility, skew and kurtosis between the SPX and NDX indices.

Making money in sports betting is just as challenging as making money in the financial markets. My enjoyment of sports made it easy for me to choose sports betting over trading in the financial markets. Being my own boss, waking up when I feel like it, watching tons of baseball, basketball and football games and traveling frequently to Las Vegas all helped tip the scale towards sports betting. You probably have similar interests in sports if you are reading this book.

Interpreting Data

I view and explain the sports-betting market as if it were a financial market by applying skill sets from my background in derivatives trading. I wrote this book from the perspective of a trader and a bettor, not from the perspective of an academic researcher. The trader/bettor looks for data that can be used to make money (or avoid losing money), and does not necessarily demand a high level of statistical significance.

Conclusions reached by research of historical sports data are results from limited sample sizes. The smaller the sample size, the less reliable the data are in predicting the future. On the other hand, results from large sample sizes are well known and usually embedded in current betting lines. Bettors who do a good job interpreting data from small sample sizes have an advantage. While reading this book, be aware of the sizes of the samples. The smaller the sample size, the greater margin of error you should associate with the results. The larger the sample size, the more you should expect the results are already reflected in current betting lines.

Legality

Taking bets on sporting events is illegal in most states in the United States. Making bets seem to be in a gray legal area. With that in mind, this book is geared towards betting in Nevada, especially Las Vegas. If you live in a country where sports betting is legal and socially accepted, consider yourself lucky.

You are more likely to get paid on a winning bet made in Nevada than anywhere else. The industry is regulated in Nevada, and there is an avenue for you to voice grievances if you feel the sportsbook has treated you unfairly. Justice may not be served all the time, but it is better than wondering how to get your money back from a tiny outfit in the Caribbean Islands.

Any wager that is made in Nevada cannot be retracted by the casino once the bet is made. This is not the case in other places, where sportsbooks sometimes cancel wagers after they are made if they feel they put up a bad line. Some notorious Internet sportsbooks have canceled wagers after a game was played, presumably due to having a big imbalance of action and their side losing! Nevada is the safest place for sports bettors.

CHAPTER 2
BASICS

This chapter goes over some basics of sports betting. All sports bettors should know the information in this chapter.

Expected Value (EV)

You are in the supermarket shopping for bread. You see two brands that you like equally, but one is cheaper. You decide to buy the cheaper one. You have just made a decision by comparing the expected value of the two brands of bread.

You are driving on a highway during rush hour. Your lane seems to be going slower than the lane to your left. The first chance you get, you switch over to the left lane so you can get home faster. You have just made a decision based on the comparison of the expected value of the two lanes.

You are at the sportsbook watching a game and the first half just ended. One team is playing without emotion and you think that will be the cause of their downfall in the second half. You decide to make a second half bet against the emotionless team based on your gut feeling. Right or wrong, you have just made a decision based on the perceived expected value of the teams.

Expected value is a concept that all people use in their daily lives, sometimes without being conscious of it. Whenever there is a choice, expected value can be useful in making a decision.

Sometimes the values are not purely monetary. The value could be based on happiness, a term that academics like to call utility.

Although often there is no need to use a formula to calculate the expected value of a decision, there are cases where a calculation gives a result that is counterintuitive, or shows why an idea is correct or incorrect. It can also help to pinpoint factors to consider in sports betting.

Expected value (EV) describes the value of an event averaged over all possible outcomes. It is a way to describe situations that can have different results. Consider a basketball player at the free throw line. If Dwayne Wade has made 750 free throws out of 1,000 attempts, a fair estimation of his chance of making his next free throw is 75%. The EV of the number of points scored with one free throw attempt is 0.75. Wade either makes the free throw and scores one point or misses the free throw and scores no points; but on average, with one free throw, he is expected to score 0.75 points. The concept of EV is used throughout this book to demonstrate the value of certain bets and ideas. This chapter introduces EV, and shows how it is calculated and how it can be used.

Calculating EV

To calculate the EV of an event, take all possible outcomes and assign each of them a monetary result and a probability. The sum of the probabilities equals 100%. The sum of the individual results, each multiplied by its probability, equals the EV of that event. If the EV of the event is a positive number, the event has a positive expectation or positive EV. If the EV of the event is a negative number, the event has a negative expectation or negative EV.

Here is an example with a roll of a single die. You roll a fair die, and each of the six faces has an equal chance of coming up. If the die comes up 1 through 4, you win $3. If the die comes up 5 or 6, you lose $3. Below are the probabilities of each roll and the results.

Face	Prob.	Result	Prob. x Result
1	1/6	+ $3	+ $0.50
2	1/6	+ $3	+ $0.50
3	1/6	+ $3	+ $0.50
4	1/6	+ $3	+ $0.50
5	1/6	- $3	- $0.50
6	1/6	- $3	- $0.50
Total	6/6	N/A	+ $1.00

The last column shows the multiplication of the Probability and the Result columns. Add all the numbers in that column to get the result, the EV of a roll: +$1. You expect to make $1 per roll of the die. But you will not win $1 on any given roll; you will either win $3 or lose $3. This information can be written as a mathematical equation:

EV of rolling one die
$$= 1/6 \times (+\$3) + 1/6 \times (+\$3) + 1/6 \times (+\$3)$$
$$+ 1/6 \times (+\$3) + 1/6 \times (-\$3) + 1/6 \times (-\$3)$$
$$= \$1.00$$

In mathematics the order of operations is to do everything within parentheses first (in this case there are no operations within parentheses), then multiply and divide, and then add and subtract. In the EV equation for rolling one die, multiply $1/6 \times (+\$3)$ to get +$0.50, and do the same for each term before adding all the terms together.

Look at another example. If the roll is a 1, you win $100; but you lose $1 with any other number. This is a great game for you, provided your opponent is not cheating. This shorter equation is simpler than writing out each term.

EV of rolling one die
$$= (1/6 \times \$100) + (5/6 \times -\$1)$$
$$= \$15.83$$

There is no need to write out each of the rolls from 2 through 6 because they all have the same result: a loss of $1. The solution for the equation is $15.83. You expect to make $15.83 on average per roll of the die. Losses outnumber wins; on average you lose five out of every six rolls. But the win amount overwhelms the loss amount by so much that you have a positive EV of $15.83 on average per roll.

Sports betting EV example

Most lines that sportsbooks offer are efficient. On most point spread wagers, the sportsbook collects the juice in that you have to risk more than you can win on a straight bet. If the bet has a 50% chance of winning, then the sportsbook has positive EV against you. Here is a sports betting EV example.

The Celtics are a 3.5 point favorite against the Knicks. The sportsbook has set a good line and there is a 50% chance of either team covering the point spread.

You go to the window and bet $110 to win $100 on the Celtics -3.5. Here is your EV on the bet if you have a 50% chance of winning it:

EV of Celtics -3.5 -110
= (50% x $100) + (50% x -$110)
= -$5

If most lines on the board are efficient, then most bets made by bettors have negative EV from the point of view of the bettors. The sportsbook has the disadvantage of not choosing which team you will bet on. But if the book sets all lines reasonably correctly, then it holds a big advantage over most gamblers.

You should try to put yourself into situations where you have positive EV. Winning requires being able to distinguish between situations with positive EV and situations with negative EV. When you find a positive-EV bet, jump on it. When you see a negative-EV bet, pass. Losing sports bettors are not able to distinguish between positive and negative EV, so they often make negative-EV bets. The goal of this book is to help you better identify positive-EV and negative-EV situations.

Square bettors (squares) are people who often make negative EV bets. Sharp bettors (sharps) are people who often make positive EV bets. Semi-sharp bettors often make the same plays as sharp bettors, but who may not have the ability or the knowledge to adjust or adapt as quickly.

Money Line

The betting line on a participant (usually a team or a person) to win an event outright is expressed in terms of money lines. Examples are: the Yankees -150 to win the game; the Mets +650 to win the National League.

If the money line is negative, you have to risk that amount in order to win 100. For example, -129 in the money line means you have to risk 129 to win 100.

If the money line is positive, you have to risk 100 to win that amount. For example, +109 in the money line means you have to risk 100 to win 109.

Converting a money line into percentage

Convert a money line into its equivalent win percentage by dividing the amount you risk by the amount your ticket will be worth if your bet wins. The ticket amount is your win plus the amount you bet.

If the money line is negative, then take the money line and divide it by itself minus 100. For example, a money line of -129 converts to 56.3%:

$$= -129 / (-129 -100)$$
$$= -129 / -229$$
$$= 56.3\%$$

If the money line is positive, then take 100 and divide it by the money line plus 100. For example, a money line of +109 is converted to 47.8%:

$$= 100 / (109+100)$$
$$= 100 / 209$$
$$= 47.8\%$$

Converting percentage into a money line

If the percentage is greater than 50%, then divide it by 100% minus itself, and multiply by -100. For example, 55% is converted to -122

$$= PERC / (100\%\text{-}PERC) \times (-100)$$
$$= 55\% / (100\%\text{-}55\%) \times (-100)$$
$$= 55\% / 45\% \times -100$$
$$= 1.22 \times -100$$
$$= -122$$

If the percentage is less than 50%, then take 100% minus itself divided by itself, then multiply by +100, then put a plus sign in front of it. For example, 45% is converted to +122

$$= (100\% - PERC) / PERC \times 100$$
$$= (100\% - 45\%) / 45\% \times 100$$
$$= 55\% / 45\% \times 100$$
$$= 1.22 \times 100$$
$$= +122$$

Exactly 50% can be expressed as both +100 and -100.

Point Spread

A point spread is an artificial adjustment to the score of an event in order to determine a winner and loser for a wager. The favorite lays points and the underdog gets points. If the point spread is -5, there are three ways to compare the favorite to the underdog:

☐ Subtract 5 points from the favorite's score and compare the result to the underdog's score.

☐ Add 5 points to the underdog's score and compare the result to the favorite's score.

☐ See how many points the favorite won by, and subtract 5 points. If the result is a negative number or the dog won outright, then the dog beat the point spread.

Sportsbooks typically put up point spreads that approximately divide the action among bettors and/or equally divide the chances of either team covering the point spread. Without any other information or opinion on the line, bettors should assume point spreads are fairly efficient. However, they are not always efficient, and this is when the smart sports bettor can take advantage of the sportsbooks.

Sportsbooks change point spreads with new information. New information can be: heavy money being bet on one side; seeing money bet by certain bettors whom the sportsbooks respect highly; news about the participants in the event (such as injuries, suspensions, etc.); and following other sportsbooks that have moved their line (called moving on air).

Once you place a bet, the terms of the bet are fixed. The point spread may change as regards new bets, but the terms of an already-made bet will stay as written. Betting sports is not the same as pari-mutuel betting in horse racing.

Point spreads have accompanying money lines as well, called the vigorish, the vig or the juice. Typically, the vig is -110; you have to risk 110 in order to win 100. Sometimes the sportsbook will have a vig different from -110; instead of adjusting the point spread, the book may adjust the vig. For example, if the sportsbook gets considerable action on the Colts -3 -110, it might change the terms to the Colts -3 -120.

Some sportsbooks offer reduced juice, some all the time and some during certain times of the week. Instead of -110 juice on point spreads, a book may offer -107 or -105. Some sportsbooks in Las Vegas offer reduced juice on the Super Bowl to attract business.

Money Lines on Dogs

A bet on the underdog money line usually is expected to lose more often than win. Rarely are you expecting that the money line is so inefficient that the market has the wrong team as the favorite. The most common exception is when the money line is close to even money.

Underdog money-line bets can be positive EV even if they lose more often than they win. It is all about value.

A way to evaluate money lines is to think of them from the same perspective as trading stocks, where you are looking to buy shares with value. To do this, convert the money line into percentage and compare to your estimate for the game. If there is a sizable difference, then you have a potential bet. For example, suppose you think the Cardinals should be a +150 (40%) underdog, but you are able to bet them at +160 (38.5%). From a stock-market perspective, you are buying shares of the Cardinals at 38.5 when you think they are worth 40; that's good value and worth a bet. You do expect to lose more often than win even though you have positive EV on this bet. When the underdog does win, you expect to get paid more than your fair share, because you think the bet has positive EV.

Removing Pushes

When a wager pushes, sportsbooks refund the amount risked back to the bettor. If it is possible for a wager to push (a tie with no winner or loser), then an adjustment is needed when converting probabilities to money lines. The total probabilities that should be considered are the probabilities of the bet being a winner or a loser; ties should be taken out. Here is an example:

Proposition wager: number of shots Shaquille O'Neal will block in tonight's game? Over/under 2 blocked shots.

You need data on the distribution of blocked shots by O'Neal. Let's assume the following distribution:

Blocks	Probability
0	10%
1	25%
2	30%
3	25%
4+	10%
Sum	100%

If O'Neal gets exactly two blocked shots, then the wager is a push. In order to correctly convert the probabilities into a money line, you should throw out the probability of a push and just compare the winners and the losers. In this case, comparing the combined probabilities of 0 or 1 blocked shot versus the combined probabilities of 3 or more blocked shots. Taking out the 30% chance of a push, leaves 70% chance the bet will be either a winner or a loser. Take the probability of each possibility in the distribution and divide by 70% to get the adjusted probability. The combined adjusted probabilities should equal 100%.

Blocks	Prob	Adjusted Prob
0	10%	14.3%
1	25%	35.7%
2	removed	
3	25%	35.7%
4+	10%	14.3%
Sum	70%	100.0%

Now add the adjusted probabilities for all the over possibilities as well as for all the under possibilities. In this case, it is 50% for each. Then convert those probabilities into money lines. In this case, both over 2 and under 2 blocked shots are 50%, so the equivalent money line is +100 for each.

Talking Cents

The total vig on both sides of a bet is called the *spread*, and is usually described in terms of cents. For a point spread of -110 on each team, the total vig is 20 cents, thus a 20-cent line. For money lines, the spread usually depends on how far away the line is from +100. Sportsbooks understand that a cent is worth less as the line gets farther from +100, so they offer wider spreads as a result.

Some sportsbooks offer 10-cent lines in baseball money lines up to a certain point. For example, they may offer 10-cent lines up to a money line of -150. For a bigger favorite than that, the spread will be bigger. Examples of this would be lines of: favorite -120, underdog +110 (10-cent line) and favorite -180, underdog +160 (20-cent line).

Spreads on prop bets usually range from 20 to 40 cents.

Bettors compare money lines by referencing the differences between them, in cents. For example, money lines of +105 and +125 are 20 cents different. Laying -150 is laying 10 cents more than laying -140.

+100 (which is the same as -100) is treated the same way 0 is treated on the number line. When comparing a line of -120 to a line of +110, first figure out the difference of -120 to +100 (20 cents) and then +100 to +110 (10 cents) to get the difference (30 cents).

There is one problem with using cents as a unit. The farther away from even money, the lower the percentage differences are for each cent difference. The 10 cents from +100 to +110 (2.38%) is a greater percentage than the 10-cent difference from +200 to +210 (1.08%). 10 cents of edge in an even money bet is better than 10 cents of edge in a +200 bet.

Half Point and Push Percentage

The value of a half point can be calculated from the push percentage. First, subtract the push percentage from 100%. Then divide the result by two. Then calculate the equivalent money line from that percentage. Lastly, subtract 100 from the money line, and you will get the value of a half point in cents. Here is an example:

In the NFL from 1989 to 2006, when the home team was a -2 to -4 favorite, it won 10.2% of the games by exactly 3 points. Converting 10.2% into the value of a half point in terms of cents:

100% - 10.2% = 89.8%
89.8% / 2 = 44.9%
44.9% converted to a money line is +122.7
taking 100 from 122.7 is 22.7, and rounding yields 23 cents

So the value of a half point from 3 to 3.5 or 3 to 2.5 is 23 cents. These three lines have the same value:

-2.5 -123
-3 +100
-3.5 +123

In order to check the work, convert the money line for -2.5 and -3.5 into percentages and find the difference. It should be exactly the same as the push percentage of 3, except for small rounding errors.

Parlay

A parlay is a bet involving two or more teams where all teams must win in order for the bet to win. To figure out the expected winning percentage of a parlay, you must know the expected winning percentage of each individual event as well as whether the events are correlated.

Let's first look at the case where there is no correlation between the events in the parlay. Here is an example of a two-team parlay with zero correlation.

Both Event A and Event B have a 50% chance of covering the point spread.

In order to win the parlay, both Event A and Event B must win. The probability of that is:

Two-team parlay winning percentage
    = Event A Win% x Event B Win%
    = 50% x 50%

= 25% or +300 in the money line

Most two-team parlays pay 13 to 5 or +260. A parlay with two events that both have a 50% chance of covering the point spread and no correlation between the two events is not an attractive bet.

If the two events are correlated, then the percentages will change depending on the degree of correlation. For example, let's say that the chances of Event A winning is perfectly correlated to the chances of Event B winning. This means that whenever Event A wins, Event B also wins and vice versa. Essentially, Event A and Event B are the same event.

Two-team parlay winning percentage with perfect correlation between the two teams

= Event A Win% x [Event B Win% given Event A wins]

= 50% x 100%

= 50% or +100 in the money line

With perfectly correlated events in the parlay, the typical pay-off odds of +260 now look profitable. But this is an extreme example. Even when two events are correlated, rarely is the correlation this strong.

Let's throw in a third event (Event C) that also has a 50% chance of covering the point spread and make it a three-team parlay. Let's also assume there is no correlation between any of the three teams.

Three-team parlay winning percentage

= Event A Win% x Event B Win% x Event C Win%

= 50% x 50% x 50%

= 12.5% or +700 in the money line

For money line parlays, sportsbooks use odds off the board instead of a set payout schedule. The vig in the parlay comes from the vig in the individual money lines.

Here is an example of a two-team parlay where the expected win percentages are not 50%. Let's say there are two teams in the parlay, one is an underdog at +300 in the money line and the other is a favorite at -150 in the money line. You decide to parlay these two teams using the money lines.

Two-team parlay using money lines

= Team X Win% x Team Y Win%

= 25% x 60%

= 15% or +567 in the money line

Teaser

A teaser is a parlay bet in which each team is given a set number of additional points. The payout odds on teasers are significantly lower than the payout odds on parlays due to the additional points. To figure out the expected winning percentage of a teaser, you must know the expected winning percentage of each individual event as well as whether the events are correlated. The same exercise can be done for teasers as they were done previously for parlays.

Here is an examples of a two-team six point teaser.

Point-spread lines: Giants -2.5; Jets +10
Six point teaser lines: Giants +3.5; Jets +16

Six points are added to the point spreads of each teams; both teams must cover the enhanced point spreads. Rules differ on what happens if any teams tie. Usually in teasers with more than two-teams, if one team ties, then the teaser is changed to a teaser with one fewer team, so a three-team teaser with a tie becomes a two-team teaser.

With a two-team teaser vig of -110, the break-even rate that the average team has to win with the additional points is about 72.4% or -262 (square root of 11/21 is 72.4%).

ROI

ROI is the acronym for Return on Investment and is expressed in percentage. ROI uses two variables: return and investment. Return is the profit on the investment. Investment is the funds that you put up to make the wager(s). ROI does not take into account the time it takes for a wager to be completed. It is possible for two investments to have the same ROI, but one investment to be superior because it takes less time to complete. The formula is:

ROI = Profit / Investment

Example:
You make 500 bets during the season. Each bet is on point spreads laying -110 juice. You risk $220 to win $200 on each bet.

500 bets at $220 per bet means the total investment is $110,000. At the end of the year, your net profit is $3,300. Your ROI is:

ROI
   = $3,300 / $110,000
   = 3.0%

Some people use ROE (return on equity) or ROR (return on risk) to mean the same as ROI. See Chapter 5 for differences between ROI and ROR as applied to scalps and middles.

A higher ROI does not necessarily mean superior performance. A bettor with a high ROI may be passing on positive-EV bets with relatively low ROI. This bettor keeps his ROI high at the expense of net profit. ROI should be viewed in conjunction with overall profits in order to see the big picture.

Expected ROI

Instead of using the known profits for the return, Expected ROI uses expected profits in the numerator. The formula is:

Expected ROI = Expected Profit / Investment

Here is an example of using expected ROI to calculate expected profits. You find a money line on the Yankees at -150 against the Angels. You bet $1,500 to win $1,000 on the Yankees. At game time, Vladimir Guerrero is scratched from the Angel lineup and the mid-market line moves to Yankees -180. Assuming -180 is now the fair line, the EV is:

EV
   = (180/280) x $1,000 + (100/280) x -$1,500
   = +$107.14

The expected profit is $107.14, and the total investment was $1,500. The expected ROI on this game at game time is:

Expected ROI
   = $107.14 / $1,500
   = 7.14%

Money Management

There are two kinds of money management: smart and stupid. The smart kind of money management deals with bet sizing to reduce the probability of going bankrupt and diversifying risk. The stupid kind of money management deals with trying to turn combinations of uncorrelated negative-EV bets into a positive-EV portfolio. Unfortunately, these two concepts get confused by gamblers because both are called "money management'.

Smart money management

How much should you bet? You have to make your own decisions on how much to bet. Your personal risk preference is just that: personal. No one can tell you perfectly how much to bet given a certain bankroll unless you tell them the exact level of your personal risk preferences. There are good tools, such as the Kelly Criterion, that will help answer the right amount to bet given a certain bankroll, but these tools need your input on the amount of risk you are willing to take, as well as the expected edge of each bet. Be true to yourself and your own risk preference and take responsibility for your bets, whether they win or lose.

Here are some general conservative steps you can take to figure out how much to bet:

Figure out your sports-betting bankroll. This is the money that can be dedicated to betting; if it is lost you will be sad, but it won't eat away at you or at your family's living expenses.

For most wagers, bet only 1% of your sports-betting bankroll. This should allow the possibility of a bad losing streak to occur without crippling your bankroll. Make sure that you are comfortable with the amount that 1% represents. If losing that amount makes you sick to your stomach, then it is too much to bet. If winning that amount does nothing for you, then maybe your bankroll is set too low.

Save the 2% bets for the best bets, the ones that have the most edge. It is often difficult to gauge the exact edge you have in sports betting. It is possible you are wrong or unlucky. Do not bet a huge percentage of your bankroll on any one bet in case you are wrong or make a mistake. Betting too much and losing can be a big detriment as it can cloud your thinking on future bets.

You can risk more if the payoff schedule has little downside. For example, middling a game has little downside if equal amounts are bet on both sides. The two risks in the game are negatively correlated, so the true risk is much smaller than the total funds used for the bets.

Betting these low percentages on individual games will mean a slow bankroll growth. But it will also minimize the risk of a disaster.

Casual bettors can afford to bet a higher percentage than professional bettors because casual bettors have other income sources that professional bettors may not have.

Stupid money management

Trying to turn bad bets into a good portfolio does not work. There are no money management schemes that can turn a combination of negative-EV bets into a positive-EV portfolio. Beginning gamblers often think up their own version of the Martingale system. I thought up this system myself when I first got out of college; but lucky for me, I never put it into play. The classic Martingale system is doubling your bet size after losing. You bet a small unit on a bet that pays close to even money. If you win, you repeat the bet. If you lose, you double the bet. The doubling allows you to win one unit when the win finally does come. To illustrate the idea, let's use hypothetical games at even money juice but with true win rates of 48% for each game.

> Rule if a bet is a winner: go back to the bet size in bet 1
> Rule if a bet is a loser: bet twice as big as the previous bet
> Bet 1: $10 to win $10
> Bet 2: $20 to win $20
> Bet 3: $40 to win $40
> Bet 4: $80 to win $80
> Bet 5: $160 to win $160
> Etc.

The gambler thinks that with this progression of bets, he is surely going to win sooner or later and eventually win the $10 in his first bet. If he can repeat it forever, he will become rich! There are two requirements:

☐ The sportsbook allows infinitely large bets
☐ You have a bankroll of infinite size

No one can satisfy these two requirements, including Bill Gates and the biggest casinos in the world. Instead, what will happen if the gambler continues to play this progression is that the gambler will eventually hit one of the two limits: either his bankroll will run out or the casino will no longer accept his wager due to its size. Since he has negative EV on each bet (remember we pegged each game as having a 48% chance of winning), the sum of the bets has negative EV.

Let's say you have $2,550 in your bankroll, and you start off making $10 bets with the odds described above. It would take 8 losing bets for you to go bankrupt ($10, $20, $40, $80, $160, $320, $640 and $1,280). The chance of you going bankrupt is small; it is only 0.5346% (52% to the 8th power) or about 1 in 200. Even though it is likely you will escape and not lose eight straight bets, the big loss that occurs when the unlikely event happens will crush you. You are not being paid appropriately for the risk you are taking. If the individual bets are negative EV, then the Martingale is a negative-EV system. Here is the calculation using the variables listed in this section.

EV of the Martingale system
= (0.5346% x -$2,550) + (99.4654% x $10)
= -$3.69

You must look for positive-EV bets. Money-management systems that turn negative-EV bets into positive-EV portfolios when the bets are not correlated do not exist.

Betting in Las Vegas

Betting sports in Las Vegas casinos may be intimidating if you do not understand the layout of sportsbooks or the semantics conventionally used at the betting window. The sportsbook can look like a stock market exchange with many numbers in lights on boards high up on the walls.

Reading the board

Sportsbooks post the betting lines on the board so you can see them easily. Some use electronic boards that are updated via computer. Others use handwritten boards that must be maintained physically. If there is a conflict between what the board shows and what the computer says, the actual betting lines are according to the computer and not as shown on the board.

Each betting option has a rotation number associated with it. Sportsbooks may not have titles on their lines; but each set of lines is distinct from another, so experienced bettors have no problem distinguishing one from another. If you are in doubt, ask the clerk at the betting window.

Lines on baseball games may look like this:

107	Rangers	+155	+1.5 -135	9.5 -110
108	Mariners	-170	-1.5 -115	9.5 -110
109	Dodgers	-125	-1.5 +120	9 -115
110	Giants	+115	+1.5 -140	9 -105

The rotation numbers are 107 for the Rangers, 108 for the Mariners, etc. The money line on the first game is Rangers +155, Mariners -170. The run-line on the first game is Rangers +1.5 -135, Mariners -1.5 -115. The total on the game is 9.5, -110 for both over and under.

Lines on football games may look like this:

201	Texas Tech	-8	-320	58
202	Baylor	+8	+260	58
203	Oklahoma State	+7 -115	+240	49 -120
204	Nebraska	-7 -105	-280	49 +100

When there is no accompanying money line listed for a point spread or total, the vig is -110 on both sides. The line on Texas Tech is -8 -110. When the accompanying point spread is different from -110, the sportsbook explicitly lists it. The accompanying money line on Nebraska -7 is -105. Money lines are typically listed next to the point spread. The money line on Oklahoma State is +240. At bigger sportsbooks, money lines are offered on most games; but when the point spread is high, many casinos do not offer money lines. When a point spread is pick 'em, there may be no money line listed since it is essentially the same as the point spread.

Making a bet

To make a sports bet in Nevada, tell the cashier the rotation number of the wager and the amount you want to risk. If instead you name the team you want to bet, the cashier will have to look for the corresponding rotation number, and that wastes time. State the amount you want to bet, and proffer that amount in cash or chips. If you want to bet the money line, you have to state that explicitly or the assumption will be that you want to bet the point spread.

Examples using the baseball and football lines above:

"202 for $550" means "I'll take Baylor +8 -110 for $550 to win $500."

"204 on the money line for $560" means "I'll take Nebraska to win the game at -280, risking $560 to win $200."

"203 Under for $200" and "204 Under for $200" both mean "I'll take Under 49 in the Oklahoma State / Nebraska game risking $200 to win $200." The total is associated with both teams in the game, and the cashier needs to punch in whether you want the Over or the Under.

"110 on the run-line for $140" means "I'll take the Giants +1.5 runs risking $140 to win $100."

"Parlay 107 and 109 for $200" means "I want to parlay the Rangers on the money line and the Dodgers on the money line, risking $200." They will tell you the exact amount the parlay pays, in this case, it should be $718.

"Parlay 109 run-line and Over for ten dimes" means "I want to parlay the Dodgers on the run-line laying 1.5 runs and Over 9 in the Dodgers / Giants game for $10,000." They will likely tell you to get lost because the items you want to bet are correlated and your bet size is high.

In Nevada once you make a bet and receive the ticket, the bet is good. Future line changes do not affect your bet. Even if the sportsbook made a ridiculous mistake, it has to honor the ticket. If a team should be favored by 33 points, but a sportsbook mistakenly allows you to bet it plus 33 points, the book has to honor your ticket when you win.

Collecting winnings

The event must end completely in order for you to collect your winnings. The date the event ends will be printed on your ticket. If you have a winner, go to the sportsbook and present the ticket. The clerk will give you the amount of your winnings plus the amount you wagered. A winning ticket risking $110 to win $100 will pay you $210. If you have another wager to make at that time, you may use the funds to make the wager without exchanging cash. Large winnings can be requested in the form of chips (chip denominations are usually $1,000, $5,000, and higher amounts) which can be used only for wagers at that sportsbook.

Winning tickets can be mailed in, and the casino will send you a check. Instructions are listed on the back of the ticket.

Tickets have expiration dates listed on the back. Generally it is 30 to 120 days after the event.

CHAPTER 3
WAYS TO WIN

There are many ways you can win at sports betting. Some people are good at handicapping games. Others are good at spotting value in a bet based on information from other lines. And still others are good at finding and betting into stale lines (lines that have not changed at one sportsbook but have at most others). Here is an overview of different ways that people win in sports betting, split into three categories:

- ☐ Handicappers
- ☐ Relative-value players
- ☐ Bettors

These categories are not mutually exclusive. Although some people concentrate on strategies in one category, many people use strategies in more than one category. Some strategies can be approached successfully from the perspectives of both handicapper and relative-value player. Both need to become bettors in order to turn picks into positive EV bets. The three categories are intertwined.

While these are methods people use in beating sportsbooks, not everyone who uses these methods will be a winner. The percentage of sports bettors who are winners is low, and losing players may often use one or more of these strategies. This overview is not an exhaustive list of all the ways people can win betting sports, but it captures many of the methods that winning players use.

Handicappers

Good handicappers can make money by betting their own picks and/or selling them. Break-even or bad handicappers can make money off their own picks only by selling them. Be wary when you listen to the radio or TV guy screaming about a five-star lock and how he is the greatest handicapper in the world; he likely only sells his picks and does not bet them.

Here are some different ways that good handicappers create their picks.

Fundamental

Fundamental handicappers look at the individual teams and players and formulate an opinion on the quality of each team. Statistics and forecasting are used to form these opinions. Some handicappers look only at the few statistics they think are important and ignore most others. Other handicappers look at every number they can get their hands on. Power ratings are often used to compare one team to another.

Angles and trends

Some handicappers look at angles and trends. Others look at angles and trends in conjunction with fundamental analysis.

An angle is an isolated idea that is relevant to the game at hand. It may be as simple as: "Old baseball players do not play as well in a day game following a night game, due to old bodies needing more time to recover." Or it could be more involved like: "Favorites on the road against a divisional rival are less likely to cover the spread due to the fatigue of traveling."

A trend is a sample of recent games that fit a pattern. The fact that the sample sizes used by trend followers are small is a big negative. For example, how much weight should be put on a trend that shows Nebraska has gone 7-1 against the spread in its last 8 games on the road as double digit favorites when off a bye week? When a data miner examines many possible trends, he is going to find a few that deviate greatly from random but won't be predictive of the future. In any set of random data, outliers exist. I do believe that some people occasionally spot trends with predictive power, but I also believe that most trends are actually random fluctuations.

Situational and emotional

Some handicappers look at special situations and figure out how the teams may be positively or negatively affected. These situations may be due to motivation and the emotions of the players involved in the game. Examples are teams that are especially motivated while their opponents are not expected to bring the same intensity to the game.

The Eagles' first game in the 2006 NFL season against the Cowboys and Terrell Owens is a good example. The Eagles as a team were especially motivated and focused on the game; they wanted revenge against their old teammate. Meanwhile the Cowboys, other than Owens, probably looked at the game as just another NFC East divisional game.

Handicapping the emotions of teams is more valuable in "physical" sports such as football and basketball. Handicapping emotions is less important in baseball, where exerting greater strength may not necessarily favor the player. Hitters who are playing more intensely than normal do not necessarily perform better than normal. Pitchers who are throwing harder may have less than normal command of the strike zone.

Feel

To handicap by feel is to examine a team and get a feeling based on what the handicapper has seen in the past. For example, a bettor may say "Peyton Manning has never won a big game in the playoffs, and he never will. I'm going to bet against the Colts because Manning will choke yet again." This is probably how most people handicap games. Of course, most people are not winning sports bettors. I am not convinced that you can beat the current sports betting market by feel alone.

Futures

Betting futures is different because the bets take a long time to be decided. It also requires a big bankroll and patience in finding favorable lines. A good futures bettor needs to handicap the teams and do a good job of projecting lines into the future. He also needs to have a solid understanding of the basic math needed for sports betting.

Relative-Value Players

Relative-value players do not need to handicap well in order to have an edge in sports betting. Instead, they use other information to help them make money. This includes the use of historical information, simulations, logic and comparable lines in different markets.

Database keepers

Database keepers have large databases of games with lines, results and other information they think is pertinent. Some database keepers use this information as part of their handicapping process. Others use this information for relative-value plays in side bets. Examples of side bets are the first half and the first quarter in football and the run line in baseball. With access to so much information, database keepers can look at historical results to figure out how the actual point spread, money line or total is related to the side bet. The bigger the sample size, the more comfortable database keepers are with their results. Database keepers invest time and/or money keeping their databases current. They have to be proficient at interpreting the data; having a good database but interpreting the data incorrectly produces negative-EV ideas and bets.

Buying points

Getting positive EV by buying points in a football or basketball game requires understanding the value of each point. Database keepers can get these values from their historical databases. You can also get these values from other sources that do not require a massive database.

Long ago, point buyers off the 3 in the NFL did well because some sportsbooks allowed bettors to buy any half point for just ten cents. When the line on an NFL game is 3, buying the dog to +3.5 or the favorite to -2.5 for just ten cents is worthwhile due to the frequency at which the favorite wins by exactly 3. Bettors could blindly bet both sides off the 3 and have positive EV. Nowadays most sportsbooks have made it more expensive to buy off the 3.

Teasers

Relative-value players can beat teasers (parlays with additional points added to each team, but with worse odds) if they have a good idea of the distributional frequency of the possible results of the game at hand. This is similar to the knowledge required for buying points. No handicapping is necessary, but with the inclusion of good handicapping, the relative-value player can add some teasers that are not as obvious or eliminate the worse teasers from his portfolio.

Handicapper/Relative-Value Overlap

Handicappers and relative-value players can arrive at the same conclusions using their particular styles of analysis. Some people can combine the skills of handicapping and relative-valuation to come up with picks. Here are some strategies where the skills of handicappers and relative-value players can overlap.

Proposition bets

There are many types of proposition bets and they can be beaten in different ways. Some can be beaten with historical or distributional information. An example is whether there will be a score in the last two minutes of the first half. With historical information, the database keeper will have no trouble coming up with an estimated value. A fundamental handicapper will have a tougher time valuing this prop.

Handicappers can beat some props just as they can beat point spreads. An example is whether Peyton Manning will throw for more than 300 yards in the Super Bowl against the Bears. This prop requires handicapping the teams and players. A database keeper will have a tougher time getting enough data to be comfortable making this analysis.

There are also some props where a person can have different thoughts depending on how they attack the problem. If that is the case, it is best to avoid making any wagers. For example, a handicapper may think that the Super Bowl usually starts off conservatively called by both coaches. Thus a field goal is more likely to be the first score of the game than in a typical NFL regular season game. On the other hand, his database may show that a touchdown is the first score more often than a field goal in a typical NFL regular season game. These two conflicting thoughts may convince the bettor to pass on the prop because his two different methods show different values on the same prop.

Parlays

A relative-value player can beat parlays by making two or more bets that are related. The higher the correlation, the greater edge there is in the parlay. You do not need to know how to handicap or have an edge on a specific side. You need to know only that the two bets have correlated results, meaning that if one wins, the other is more likely to win than to lose.

A handicapper who can expect to beat the point spread at a 53% or higher clip is a winning handicapper. As the expected winning percentage increases, the handicapper gets more and more edge in playing parlays, even if the bets are not correlated. A person who is both a good handicapper and a good relative-value player can draw from both to maximize EV.

Bettors

Line hunters

Line hunters search sportsbooks for lines that may be different than the general marketplace. They do not need to handicap to win; rather, they win by jumping on weak lines. For example, if the line at a sharp sportsbook on the Jets at the Packers is Jets +3.5, line hunters would be looking for Packers -3 or Jets +4. Line hunters look for stale lines or sportsbooks fading lines. These sportsbooks that fade their lines may be getting more action on a particular team, motivating them to shade their line differently than the rest of the sports betting marketplace. They are more focused on balancing their action due to the bets they have already taken. This is when line hunters can step in and take advantage.

Line hunting in Las Vegas is difficult for an individual because it takes time to travel from one sportsbook to another. The walking distance between the large casinos on the strip seems to get longer every year with the addition of new shops and tourist attractions. In the summertime, walking between books is more difficult due to the heat. The traffic has gotten worse every year, making driving from one casino to another more difficult. Included with the driving time is the time spent parking and walking from the parking garage to the sportsbook, which can be ten minutes at some casinos.

Line hunters have the help of services that present the lines of games at various sportsbooks. However, there is no guarantee that the lines will remain unchanged. The sportsbook may have changed the line during the time it takes the bettor to get there.

Followers

Followers are bettors who bet other people's picks. Followers follow the advice of a handicapper and bet on the games that the handicapper releases. This sounds simple, but followers need to be intelligent in order to profit from their activity. They need to handicap the handicapper. Following a bad handicapper is negative EV; following a good handicapper is positive EV. Handicapping the handicapper is not as simple as just looking at the handicapper's record. Good luck or bad luck may have distorted the handicapper's record, and it is up to the followers to try to separate luck and skill and follow a handicapper with positive-EV picks.

Bonus hunting

When Internet sportsbooks were popular, bonus hunting was a favorite activity of some bettors. Bettors did not need to beat the sportsbook to make money. All they had to do on the teams they selected to bet was break even or play with a small negative EV. The expectation was that the bonus from the Internet sportsbook would be enough to cover the expected small losses.

Here is a typical arrangement: The sportsbook would give a certain percentage of your deposit as a bonus. If the bonus percentage was 20%, the sportsbook would credit an extra 20% to your account. If the bonus percentage was 20%, the sportsbook would credit $100 to your account for a $500 deposit. The caveat was that you had to play the initial deposit a certain amount of times, called a rollover rate. If the rollover rate was 10 times, then you had to play $5,000 worth of plays ($500 x 10) in order to keep your bonus if you made a withdrawal. Early withdrawal voided the bonus. $100 of bonus on $5,000 of plays is 2%, so you had the expectation of winning money provided your plays would do no worse than lose at 2%.

Promotions

Sportsbooks sometimes offer special promotions to entice you to play. Bonuses are one type of promotion, but there are other promotions as well. Promotions I have seen include free plays, better parlay odds, reduced vigorish lines, free food, and entry into a lottery for a new car or house. Some of these promotions are worth enough that one does not need to be a winning handicapper to get an edge. Promotions vary, so examine the wording of the details carefully.

Betting For a Living is Work

Making money gambling is tough. Wanting to win is not enough; you must be dedicated to winning. You must be a motivated self-starter willing to work on your own time without an outside force encouraging you. It is not easy getting motivated on a daily basis. My estimate is that less than 1% of people who try to make a living gambling are actually successful within two years. A good thing about sports betting is that you do not have to do it full time to succeed. You can hold a regular job and spend your extra time on analysis and betting. If you concentrate on one segment of sports betting (such as one conference in college basketball), then betting sports does not have to consume 40 hours a week. Here are some qualities you need to succeed:

Talent

Whether it is math skills, street smarts or intuitive logic, you need talent to succeed.

Managing finances

You must understand the right amount to bet per game given your bankroll. If starting off on a good streak causes you to over-estimate your true skill, you might soon be playing too big for your bankroll. When the inevitable losing streaks hits, as it always does for everyone, your bankroll may not be able to handle the negative deviation if your bets are too big. If you know how to manage your bankroll and understand the risks you are taking, you can better handle the negative swings.

You can't be a successful sports bettor if you have a gambling problem. Problem gamblers bet more than they can afford to lose. Whether it is in one game or in a series of games, they extend their bankrolls to the limit and sometimes beyond. In order to succeed in sports betting, you must be able to control yourself and bet within the limits of your bankroll.

Motivation after winning

When on a winning streak, it is easy to get complacent and take unscheduled days off. Are you going to be motivated to find the edge in a small bet after raking in a huge win? Are you willing to continue to grind it out on a daily basis after hitting a jackpot? If not, you will have problems motivating yourself after wins.

Motivation after losing

When on a losing streak, it is easy to stay in bed all day feeling sorry for yourself for suffering the bad beats. Why bother spending hours working on a database or walking in the Las Vegas heat when it seems you keep losing on silly last-second plays? Are you going to be motivated to gain small edges in wagers even after losing a few of them in a row?

Willingness to study

Winning sports bettors have to analyze, study and think about the games as they evolve. Line makers and other sports bettors are quick to adapt to changes, so you must keep pace or better yet, stay one step ahead of them. Reading this book is a good step toward that goal.

Persistence and physical endurance

Gambling is not the easy life that many think it is. For the Las Vegas bettor, it can mean walking 10 miles a day from sportsbook to sportsbook in 100-degree heat.

55% Wins is Great

From my experience in sports betting, I have observed few handicappers that can truly expect to win at a 55% rate or higher in the long run against widely available lines (lines that are easy to find and bet). Any handicapper who can pick at that rate over a large sample size is a truly talented handicapper and among the best in the world. The touts who claim to have winning percentages of 70% or higher are exaggerating. See Chapter 21 for more information on how to evaluate handicappers.

Table 1 shows what different win percentages yield for 1,000 wagers of $1,100 each with -110 vig. For example, the 55% win rate makes $55,000.

If it was easy to win at a 55% rate, then many people would be doing it and hurting the sportsbooks. Even with all the square bettors losing their money, sooner or later, the 55% winners would bankrupt the sportsbooks. The mere existence of -110 lines argues against there being many people who pick at a 55% rate. Based on

Table 1
Profit on 1000 Bets at Various Win Rates

Win %	Lose %	Wins	Losses	Profit
50%	50%	$500,000	-$550,000	-$50,000
51%	49%	$510,000	-$539,000	-$29,000
52%	48%	$520,000	-$528,000	-$8,000
53%	47%	$530,000	-$517,000	$13,000
54%	46%	$540,000	-$506,000	$34,000
55%	45%	$550,000	-$495,000	$55,000
56%	44%	$560,000	-$484,000	$76,000
57%	43%	$570,000	-$473,000	$97,000
58%	42%	$580,000	-$462,000	$118,000
59%	41%	$590,000	-$451,000	$139,000

knowledge of the sports betting market, experience betting sports, and logic, I have come to the conclusion that a 55% long-run win rate is not achievable for most bettors.

Bet Those 53% Games!

The sportsbooks are smart and adjust to bets from sharp bettors. You do not need to hit 55% in order to win big. A 53% winner can have a profitable activity in sports betting. More handicappers can win at 53% than at the vaunted 55%.

Winning at 54% can be better than winning at 55%. How? It is possible if the 54% winner makes more bets. Here is an example:

Assume there are two bettors who can each pick 300 bets per year that win at a 55% rate. Assume they can each pick another 300 bets that win at a 53% rate. One bettor decides to only bet the games that have a win rate of 55%. The other bettor decides to bet all plays that he expects to win at 53% or better.

Here are the results of the handicapper who bets only the 55% plays. Betting $550 to win $500 per game over 300 games means he expects to make $8,250 overall.

Win %	Lose %	Win $	Lose $	Profit
55%	45%	$82,500	-$74,250	$8,250

Here are the results of the handicapper who bets the 300 plays that he expects to win at a 55% rate, and also bets another 300 plays that he expects to win at a 53% rate. He bets $550 to win $500 per game over 600 total games. He expects to make $10,200, or $1,950 more than the first bettor.

	Win %	Lose %	Win $	Lose $	Profit
	55%	45%	$82,500	-$74,250	$8,250
	53%	47%	$79,500	-$77,500	$1,950
total	54%	46%	$162,000	-$151,800	$10,200

The bettor who passes on the 53% games is missing out on profitable situations. Although the winning percentage of a bettor is important, it is more important to consider the expected profits (assuming the additional risk is accounted for). The second bettor will have a lower win rate and a lower ROI, but will make more money. It is incorrect to look at just the winning percentage; the total number of plays in the record needs to be considered as well.

CHAPTER 4 SPORTS- BETTING MARKET

The sports-betting market is similar to financial markets. Sportsbooks act like market makers and professional traders. Sharp bettors act like hedge funds and smart investors. They can act like market makers in some instances. Square bettors act like square investors by buying high and selling low. This chapter explains how the sports-betting market works, how lines open and move, the efficiency of the market and ways to use market prices intelligently.

Not an Exchange

Unlike the stock market in the United States, there are no central exchanges or mechanisms to prevent "trade-throughs," a term used for a trade that happens at a worse price than the best bid or best offer. But there are other markets where individual entities make trades directly with each other rather than through a central clearing system like an exchange. In some markets, banks act as market makers and make bids and offers on financial products. Different banks may have different prices on the same product, but they are not obligated to tell their customers when another bank has a more competitive price. This is similar to how sportsbooks act.

All sportsbooks have betting lines on the same games, but sometimes their prices differ. If you want to bet Seattle -3 -110, the sportsbook has no obligation to tell you that you can bet Seattle -2.5 -105 across the street. You have to look at multiple sportsbooks to determine the best places to make your wagers. Comparing lines is difficult in Las Vegas since it takes time to physically travel from one sportsbook to another. Updated lines at selected sportsbooks are available on the Internet.

Goals of a Sportsbook

A sportsbook has two goals when it puts up a line: maximize profits and minimize risk. Those two goals can conflict at times, and different sportsbooks put different priorities on them.

Some sportsbooks are more risk averse and strive for minimal risk. Their casinos think of them like $5.99 buffets: useful for attracting customers but not for making profits.

Other sportsbooks are more aggressive; their primary goal is to maximize profits. These sportsbooks are willing to take unbalanced positions, and have a rooting interest on some games.

How Lines Open

Sportsbooks post new lines with a combination of the goals listed above in mind. They may have their own in-house line makers or they may subscribe to a service that sends recommendations on opening lines.

Some sportsbooks have confidence in their handicapping ability, and are not averse to posting new lines as early as they can, with reduced limits. They have the advantage of being among the few sportsbooks with lines available for betting, and they get a large market share during this early stage. Often their early lines are efficient. But when they do make mistakes, smart bettors are quick to take advantage. Lines are then adjusted to reflect the betting action. The limits are raised when the sportsbooks have a better grasp of what the efficient line should be with information they received from early betting action. The winnings of smart bettors against early lines can be considered part of the sportsbooks' costs of making the lines.

Other sportsbooks wait until lines have been bet into and adjusted at the more aggressive sportsbooks to help them decide what numbers to post.

Why Lines Move

Once lines are open, there are many reasons for sportsbooks to move them. Sportsbooks can independently move their lines for any reason, including:

- ☐ Taking big action on one side
- ☐ Seeing a sharp bettor bet on one side and having the desire to be on that same side
- ☐ Breaking news concerning players and/or teams such as injuries or lineup changes
- ☐ A changing weather forecast
- ☐ Seeing the lines move at other sportsbooks (called moving on air)

Increased interest and betting activity in any event leads to a higher chance of sportsbooks moving their lines. More line movements allow for the increased possibility of different lines at different sportsbooks. This gives line hunters more opportunity to take advantage of differing lines. Popular sports with high betting activity are often the sharp bettor's favorite sports due to the high number of opportunities caused by the general interest from squares. In high-volume sports, middlers and scalpers act similar to arbitragers in the financial markets by taking advantage of pricing differentials between sportsbooks.

Sportsbooks in Nevada can only take bets; they cannot act as customers and make bets. (Individuals such as owners of casinos and sportsbook managers may make bets at other casinos.) Thus Nevada sportsbooks cannot lay off any of their action with other sportsbooks. The only way they can try to adjust their positions is by moving their lines. In comparison, market makers in financial markets must make markets in their particular products, but they are free to trade in other markets. They can use other products to hedge their exposure, possibly allowing them to make bigger markets in their own products. For example, options market makers can hedge with underlying products (in equity options, the underlying product is the stock) to reduce their risk.

Nevada sportsbooks cannot be proactive; they can be only reactive. This may mean lower limits in Nevada. Sportsbooks outside of Nevada may not be under the same restrictions and may be free to make bets with other sportsbooks. Perhaps this is one of the factors that makes the sportsbooks at the multi-billion-dollar casinos in Nevada smaller than some outfits elsewhere.

Lines can be adjusted at any time, but generally in major sports, they seem to move the most early and late. Lines move early if they are weak and taken advantage of by sharp bettors. Lines move late when sportsbooks accept huge bets on one side and want to attract action on the other side.

In the past, once the game started, the betting action was over. With the advent of in-game trading and halftime betting, markets may still be active even after a game starts. Only when the game or event ends does the market truly close.

Game-to-Game Line Adjustment

Line adjustments made from one game to another are often subtle and difficult to detect since many variables change from game to game. Here is an example of a line change where the variables stayed the same, so the main reason for the line change was adjustment to the marketplace. The sportsbook opened an overnight baseball line at home team -160. A couple of sharp bettors each bet large on the road team, so the sportsbook adjusted the line to -140; 20 cents is a big move in baseball. Then the game was canceled due to rain, and rescheduled for the following day. Sports bets are good only for the day stated on the ticket; so all bets made on the canceled game were void, even though the same teams and pitchers were rescheduled for the following day. The rescheduled game opened at home team -140. The -160 may have been a mistake, but the line maker learned from the market reaction and did not make the same mistake the following day.

Different Markets

There are sub-markets in sports betting. Each sport can be categorized in a sub-market. The different types of bets that are offered in each sport can be categorized further into minor sub-markets. Some of these markets have a lot of interest from bettors, while others do not. The market in NFL games is the deepest and most active market in American sports betting, with NFL point spreads leading the way. Within the NFL betting market there are niche markets such as prop lines, lines on individual quarters, and Grand Salami lines (lines on the combined score of all road teams versus the combined score of all home teams).

Typically the betting limits and the volatility of line movements are related to the size of the market. For example, limits on Arena football may be $500 at a major sportsbook, and the lines move on a $500 wager. But the limits at the same sportsbook on an NFL game might be $100,000, and a four-figure wager may not budge the line.

Having an edge in a big market like NFL point spreads has more value than having an equivalent edge in a small market like Arena football point spreads. You can bet a lot more in one market than the other. Small bettors in small markets need to keep this in mind as well because their growth potential is limited.

Efficiency of Sports-Betting Markets

The efficient-market theory says it is difficult or impossible to beat the market with public information. There are different levels of efficiency, ranging from strong to weak. The strong form of the theory says investors can not consistently generate greater-than-average market returns based on public information, and that the current market price reflects all public information about the asset. The weak form of the theory says that most public information is reflected in the current market price, but it is possible for some people to generate excess profits because markets are not completely rational all the time. While a good estimate of the value of any asset is its current market price, it is possible for someone to correctly think it is overvalued or undervalued. The weak-form of the theory seems to work well in describing most financial markets and also works well in describing the sports-betting market.

Most lines in sports betting are efficient. It is the few lines that are inefficient that allow bettors to make bets with positive EV. Without a central marketplace, sportsbooks may make the mistake of offering lines that the bettor can arbitrage. Sharp bettors have a slight edge on a number of profitable plays, but not enough to hurt the sportsbooks' overall business since there are so many more square bettors than sharp bettors.

The efficiency of any sports-betting market depends on two things:

☐   the ratio of square money to sharp money
☐   comparative knowledge between line makers and sharp bettors

When the market is not efficient, it is often due to squares betting on the negative EV side. In situations when the ratio of the square bettor's money to sharp bettors' money is high, sportsbooks shade their lines to increase profit and/or reduce risk. Shading lines too much gives opportunity to the sharp bettors.

In financial markets, higher volume and more trading interest usually mean more efficient markets; but this is not as often the case in sports betting. Lines on important NFL games can be more inefficient than regular season MLB games even though there is much more money bet on the NFL game. For example, Super Bowl lines can be inefficient because the ratio of square bettors' money to sharp bettors' money is high. Many square bettors come out of the woodwork to bet on the Super Bowl. Meanwhile, the number of sharp bettors stays the same whether it is the middle of the season or the Super Bowl. Super Bowl lines are likely to be less efficient than regular-season lines.

Other inefficiencies arise when the knowledge of sharp bettors is greater than the knowledge of line makers. This can happen in sports where there is less interest like Arena Football, NFL Europe and the WNBA. Big line moves are an indication of inefficient opening lines; in general, minor sports see bigger line moves than major sports. If you have interest in a minor sport, you likely will find betting opportunities in your sport. You won't be able to bet as much as you could on an NFL game.

Relative-Value Bets

Efficient game lines can help value wagers in other similar markets from a relative-value point of view. If there are two related markets one of which is efficient, then you can use the efficient market to value the line in the other market. Some examples are NFL first half lines compared to NFL game lines, Super Bowl proposition bets adjusted for the total in the game, and NBA exact series lines calculated on expected individual game lines. Another name for relative-value bets is derivative bets because their valuations are derived from efficient lines in another market.

Zero-Sum Game

Sports betting is a zero-sum game; the combined profits and losses by all participants equal zero (ignoring expenses like taxes and casino employee wages). When someone wins, someone else has to lose.

Sharp bettors can beat sportsbooks by betting into inefficient lines. To the extent that there are not enough bets on the other side, sportsbooks are footing the EV of sharp bettors. Sportsbooks are not happy to take unbalanced big bets from bettors identified as sharp. But sportsbooks may be happy to take sharp action if it helps balance their risk. In that case, sharp bettors are beating square bettors indirectly, and both sharp bettors and sportsbooks are rooting for the same side. Square bettors make up the negative side of the zero-sum equation that allows sportsbooks and sharp bettors to both make money. Thus square bettors can be viewed as the driving force in the sports-betting market.

Market Value in Finance

In the financial markets, "marking to market" is the act of assigning a fair value to stocks and other financial assets. Usually the fair value price is the price of the closing trade of the day. This price is used to value investments to find the current market value of portfolios.

The concept of market value is also useful in evaluating sports wagers. It allows the user to determine the actual risk in the wager for a particular game. It also allows the user to compare one bet to another for relative-value plays and is useful for hedging purposes.

It is not used enough by sports bettors and many fall into a trap of not understanding the true risk of their wagers.

In the financial markets, the market value of an investment (MVFinancial) is simply the price times the number of shares owned.

MVFinancial = Current Price x Shares

If you own 100 shares of IBM, and the current price is $50, then the market value of your shares is $5,000 ($50 x 100). The market value of your shares is the same whether their cost was $10 per share or $60 per share.

Market Value in Sports Bets

Calculating the market value of a sports wager (MVSports) is similar. The "Current Price" is replaced by the probability of the ticket winning. The "Shares" is replaced by the amount you get back if the wager is a winner. The amount you get back includes the initial wager as well as the winnings because the sportsbook keeps your initial wager and does not return it unless you win your bet. (To do otherwise is called "credit betting," and there is no credit betting in Nevada). The market value of a sports wager is the probability of the ticket winning times the amount you get back.

MVSports
    = Probability of Ticket Winning x Amount you get back

Example with a Super Bowl futures bet

Here is an example using a Super Bowl futures bet. Before the 2006 NFL season, you made a wager on Seattle to win Super Bowl XL at 20-1 for $100. Your wager, assuming you made it at a fair market price, had a market value (MV0) of $100 at the time you made it.

MV0
    = Probability of Seattle winning Super Bowl x Amount you collect if you win
    = 1/21 x $2,100 = $100

During the season, every game that had an impact on the probability of Seattle winning the Super Bowl had an impact on the market value of your ticket. If a win by Seattle gave it a greater shot at the #1 seed in the NFC, then that win increased the market value of your ticket. When Seattle clinched the NFC West division, the probability of winning the Super Bowl increased, and the market value of your ticket increased. When Seattle won its first playoff game, both the probability of Seattle winning the Super Bowl and the market value of your ticket increased.

Now let's fast forward to the day before the Super Bowl. The market shows the probability of Seattle winning the game is 37%. Here is the market value (MV1) of your futures bet on the day before the Super Bowl:

MV1: 37% x $2,100 = $777

The market value of your ticket is now $777. If you were to sell that ticket to someone on the day before the Super Bowl, a fair price would be $777. Your initial investment was $100, so you have already theoretically won $677.

The market value of your wager tells you how much money you have at risk. If Seattle loses in the Super Bowl, you will lose $777 in market value; your ticket value goes from $777 to $0. It is incorrect to think that if Seattle loses the game you lose only the $100 that you originally bet. As of the day before the Super Bowl, you had already won $677 with your ticket since its market value went from $100 to $777.

On the other hand, if Seattle wins the Super Bowl, the market value of your ticket goes from $777 to $2,100. You did not win $2,000 on the Super Bowl itself, but instead you won only an additional $1,323 ($2,100 - $777). You get back $2,100 when you cash in your winning ticket ($2,000 you won plus the $100 that you gave the sportsbook to make the initial wager), but the market value of the ticket was already $777 before the game.

The key to determining the market value of the ticket is marking to the current fair market price. Finding the fair market value can be done by looking at futures odds at sportsbooks and sports betting exchanges, as well as doing your own analysis.

Seattle was an example of a team that increased its chances of winning the Super Bowl throughout the season, and the futures ticket increased in value. All of that value collapsed to zero when Seattle lost the Super Bowl. It was a roller coaster ride. The market value of the ticket went from $100 slowly up to $777 right before the Super Bowl. Then it collapsed from $777 to $0 when Seattle lost the game.

Example of a bad team

Let's take a look at a bad team. Oakland lost its first three games of the 2006 NFL season. With each loss, Oakland's chances of winning the Super Bowl worsened. Let's assume before the regular season began, the probability of Oakland winning the Super Bowl was 2.94%, with fair odds of 33-1. You made a $100 wager on Oakland at those odds. Let's also assume that after each of the first three losses, the probability of Oakland winning the Super Bowl decreased to 1.5%, 0.8% and 0.3% respectively.

The market values before the regular season and after each of their first three games were as follows:

MV0: 2.94% x $3,400 = $100
MV1: 1.5% x $3,400 = $51
MV2: 0.8% x $3,400 = $27
MV3: 0.3% x $3,400 = $10

In the first game, you lost $49 ($100-$51) in value on the ticket. You lost another $24 in the second game and another $17 on the third game.

After the third game of the season, Oakland has such a small chance to win the Super Bowl that your original wager has already lost most of its original value. When Oakland was finally mathematically eliminated from the playoff race, it came as no surprise and the drop in market value in that last game was tiny. By that time it was inevitable that Oakland would not make the playoffs and the market value of your ticket was already close to $0.

In the case of Oakland, it was not the 11th or 12th game of the season (or whichever game it was that mathematically eliminated the team from the playoffs) that made your ticket go from a value of $100 to $0; it was a series of games before that one. Losing the first game of the year dropped the market value by almost half. If the above probabilities of Oakland winning the Super Bowl after each game are correct, then the game where your ticket lost the most value was the first game. If Oakland had won its second and third games, then the value of the ticket would have bounced back to match the increased probability of Oakland winning the Super Bowl.

Example of analyzing your risk

Let's say it is the eleventh week of the season, and the Broncos are playing the Chargers. This is a big game for both teams as the winner will have a big leg up on winning the division, including tiebreaker scenarios. Before the season began, you bet $100 on the Broncos to win the AFC West at 2 to 1. Here are your estimates for the Broncos to win the AFC West before and after the game versus the Chargers.

> Your estimates for the Broncos to win the AFC West
> Before the game: 40%
> If the Broncos beat the Chargers: 60%
> If the Chargers beat the Broncos: 20%

The line on the game is pick 'em. You know a sportsbook that is offering the Chargers at even money, and another sportsbook that is offering the Broncos at even money. This means you may increase your position, or hedge out of your position (for this game only) without having to pay any juice.

In order to analyze your true risk on the game, figure out the market value of your ticket before the game, what the market value will be if the Broncos win, and what the market value will be if the Broncos lose. Given the information above, the market values are:

> MV before game: (40% x 300) + (60% x 0) = $120
> MV if Broncos win: (60% x 300) + (40% x 0) = $180
> MV if Broncos lose: (20% x 300) + (80% x 0) = $60

If the Broncos win, the market value on your futures bet increases from $120 to $180 for a net gain of $60. If the Broncos lose, the market value on your futures bet decreases from $120 to $60 for a net loss of $60.

Your true risk is +$60 if the Broncos win and -$60 if the Broncos lose. It should be clear that the perfect hedge is to bet $60 on the Chargers at even money. That would reduce your risk to zero with a zero EV bet. Not all examples are as simple as this. See chapter 6 for more on this issue.

Notice that the EV of the game is zero. It should be zero because you have marked your position on the Broncos future at fair value.

EV = (Prob. Broncos win x increase in MV)
    + (Prob. Broncos lose x decrease in MV)
= (50% x +60) + (50% x -60)
= $0

Why Mark to Market?

Marking to market is crucial when considering hedging. Knowing the current market value allows you to figure out the true risk of your bets and thus it allows you to figure out the perfect hedge. This topic is discussed in detail in chapter 6.

Marking to market is an important factor for relative-value plays. Relative-value players compare different bets to see if there are inconsistencies. Marking to market allows you to make comparisons in bets like futures, props and other type of bets that are closely related to the point spread or total.

CHAPTER 5
SCALPING &
MIDDLING

Scalping

A scalp is a combination of two bets that are mirror images of each other. The combination of the two bets in a perfect scalp has zero risk and you win the same amount no matter the outcome of the event. Scalps might consist of bets that are other than perfect mirror images of each other; they may slightly favor one side over the other.

Perfect scalp

Here is an example of a perfect scalp with no risk remaining. The Lakers are playing at the Spurs.

Bet 1: Lakers +3.5 +100, risking $100 to win $100
Bet 2: Spurs -3.5 +110, risking $95.24 to win $104.76

If the Lakers cover the +3.5 point spread, your result will be:

Lakers +3.5 +100 Win +$100
Spurs -3.5 +110 Lose -$95.24
Total Result: +$4.76

If the Spurs cover the -3.5 point spread, your result will be:

Lakers +3.5 +100 Lose -$100
Spurs -3.5 +110 Win +$104.76
Total Result: +$4.76

No matter who covers the spread, the Lakers or the Spurs, your total result is the same, a profit of $4.76 on the two bets combined. This is a perfect scalp; there is no risk remaining, and you are indifferent on who covers the spread.

Imperfect scalp

Here is an example of an imperfect scalp with minimal risk remaining. The Suns are playing at the Heat.

Bet 1: Suns -4.5 +100, risking $100 to win $100
Bet 2: Heat +4.5 +110, risking $100 to win $110

This is a more practical scalp because betting $100 at the sportsbook is more natural and less cumbersome than betting $95.24.

If the Suns cover the -4.5 point spread, your result will be:
Suns -4.5 +100 Win +$100
Heat +4.5 +110 Lose -$100
Total Result: $0

If the Heat covers the +4.5 point spread, your result will be:
Suns -4.5 +100 Lose -$100
Heat +4.5 +100 Win +$110
Total Result: +$10

There is a little bit of risk remaining in the scalp; you are slightly better off if the Heat cover the spread. But even if the Suns cover the spread, you do not lose anything. This is a scalp, just not a perfect one.

Negative scalp

A negative scalp is a scalp that is guaranteed to lose. Generally sports bettors are not interested in negative scalps, but they can happen sometimes. Here is an example of an intentional negative scalp:

Baylor is playing Texas Tech in basketball. You handicap the game with Baylor -3 as the correct line. The game opens at Baylor pick 'em -110 and you decide to make a wager.

Later in the day, before the game starts, you hear news that two star players for Baylor were just suspended for the game by the coach for curfew infractions. You know this is a big impact and without these two star players, you think the line really should be Texas Tech -1.5. You quickly run to the closest sportsbook and see that the line has not moved. They still have the game at pick 'em, but you have to lay -110 to bet either Baylor or Texas Tech. You decide to bet Texas Tech -110, which has a slight positive EV if the true line is Texas Tech -1.5. Normally you would not make that bet because the line is too close to your handicapping expectations and there is not enough room for error. In this case though, given you have new information and you already have a bet on the "wrong" team, a bet on Texas Tech makes sense because it has positive EV and reduces your risk.

The two bets combined is a negative scalp. No matter who wins, you will lose 10 cents due to the juice. But you do think locking into the negative 10 cents is a better alternative to letting the original wager ride. The negative scalp was intentional, and it will decrease your expected loss, and that is a good thing.

Middling

A middle is a combination of two bets that are closely related, but not exactly mirror images of each other. The combination of the two bets still has risk remaining, but usually is less risky than having just one side naked. Middles are riskier than scalps, but the potential rewards are higher. Typically a middle provides a big win if the event lands on a perfect number or a few perfect numbers, depending on the size of the middle. The risk is that if the game does not land on a perfect number, then you lose a small amount.

Example of a middle

The Jets are playing at the Raiders.

Bet 1: Jets -2.5 -110, risking $110 to win $100.
Bet 2: Raiders +3.5 -120, risking $120 to win $100

You believe the correct line is Jets -3 -100. You also believe there is a 10% chance that the Jets will win by exactly 3 points. Therefore, you believe the Jets have a 45% chance of winning by more than 3, and the Raiders have a 45% chance of covering +2.5.

Here is your expected probability table and possible results.

Result of Game	Prob.	Jets	Raiders	sum
Jets win by 4 or more	45%	+$100	-$120	-$20
Jets win by exactly 3	10%	+$100	+$100	+$200
Raiders cover +2.5	45%	-$110	+$100	-$10

If the Jets win by exactly 3, then you win both bets. Any other outcome means you lose one side and win the other. Since you are paying the juice on both bets, winning one and losing the other will give you a small loss. These two bets should be looked at as a tandem. The true risk is whether or not the Jets will win by exactly three. Here is the EV calculation of the two bets given the probability distribution shown in the table above.

The EV of the two bets combined equals:
= (45% x -$20) + (10% x +$200) + (45% x -$10)
= +$6.50

If your expectation of the probability distribution of the game is correct, then you have a positive-EV middle. Unfortunately, 90% of the time you will lose small. But the other 10% of the time, you will win big. The big wins will cover the losses by a nice margin if your probability distribution is on target. If your numbers are incorrect, you may have a negative-EV middle.

Half middle

A half middle is a middle where one or both bets are on a full point spread number instead of a half point. The game can potentially land on a number where one side wins but the other side is a push.

Here is an example of a half middle. The Bears are playing the 49ers.

Bet 1: Bears -2.5 -105, risking $105 to win $100
Bet 2: 49ers +3 -105, risking $105 to win $100

If the Bears win by exactly 3 points, you win the bet on Bears -2.5 and push on the bet on the 49ers +3. Here is a table with a probability distribution and results.

Result of Game	Prob.	Bears	49ers	sum
Bears win by 4 or more	45%	+$100	-$105	-$5
Bears win by exactly 3	10%	+$100	$0	+$100
49ers cover +2.5	45%	-$105	+$100	-$5

The EV of the two bets combined equals:
= (45% x -$5) + (10% x +$100) + (45% x -$5)
= +$5.50

Reverse middle

A reverse middle is the opposite of a middle. In a reverse middle, you are hoping the game does not land in the middle of two different numbers. A middle by itself is not a profitable bet. Profitability depends on the point spread, the odds, and the probability of the game landing on certain numbers. This means it is possible for the other side of the middle — a reverse middle — to be profitable.

Here is an example of a reverse middle with positive EV. The Knicks are playing the Bulls.

Bet 1: Knicks -5.5 +100, risking $100 to win $100
Bet 2: Bulls +5 +110, risking $100 to win $110

The only way you lose with this combination of bets is if the Knicks win by exactly 5 points. If the Knicks win by exactly 5 points, you lose the bet on Knicks -5.5 and push on the bet on the Bulls +5. In this example, if you assume the Knicks will win by exactly 5 points 4% of the time, then the combination of the two bets has positive EV. Here are the probability distribution and results.

Result of Game	Prob.	Knicks	Bulls	sum
Knicks win by 6 or more	48%	+$100	-$100	$0
Knicks win by exactly 5	4%	-$100	$0	-$100
Bulls cover +4.5	48%	-$100	+$110	+$10

The EV of the two bets combined equals:
$$= (48\% \times \$0) + (4\% \times -\$100) + (48\% \times \$10)$$
$$= +\$0.80$$

The reverse middle has a positive EV of +$0.80. The reverse middle does seem riskier than a middle because the reverse middle has the chance of losing big. Most people avoid reverse middles because they cannot stand to lose big if the game ends in the middle. If the situation is profitable, then sharp bettors should be able to take advantage of the reverse middle by correctly sizing their bets to fit within their own risk parameters.

Sometimes sportsbooks unavoidably have reverse-middle positions when they move lines and take bets on both sides. Players with their combined middle position have positive EV against a sportsbook in some games. But often the vig on both sides allow a sportsbook's reverse middle position to be profitable but risky.

Similarities

Scalpers and middlers engage in similar activities. Some of their thought processes and techniques are the same. Some of the risks they face are the same. Here are some of the similarities between scalpers and middlers.

☐ The risk in their wagers is minimized or eliminated.

☐ Both are voracious line hunters. They are always looking for sportsbooks with weak lines or lines that differ from the rest of the market.

☐ Both benefit if they can correctly anticipate line moves.

☐ Both face the risk of getting both bets down. It is possible they will bet one side, but not be able to bet the other side at the expected price. If the line moves as they are getting to a sports-book, they may be left naked with the initial wager without being able to bet the second wager at the expected price.

Scalpers and middlers need two different lines on the same event in order to gain positive EV. Thus they are always seeking places and ways to find these different numbers.

Line hunting gets them different numbers at different sports-books at the same time. Often the theoretical underpinnings behind a sports wager take a back seat to actually making the bet in the real world. Anyone would be happy to enter into a positive-EV scalp, but executing the scalp is the difficult part.

Anticipating line moves allows them to get different numbers (at the same or different sportsbook) at different times. If the line does not move as they anticipate, then they are left naked with just the original bet.

Differences

Even with all the similarities, there are still some differences between scalpers and middlers.

☐ Middlers need to have a good understanding of the probability a game will land on certain numbers; scalpers do not.

☐ Middlers have risk after the bets are made; scalpers do not.

☐ Middlers usually put themselves in the position to win big, but lose small. Scalpers cannot win big; they win only small. But if they scalp perfectly, they cannot lose.

Other Issues

When you find an attractive opportunity to scalp or middle, decide which side is the tougher bet to get down, and then bet that side first if possible. If you bet the easy-to-find side first, then there is some chance the tough side will not be available when you get to the sportsbook. It is also possible that the tough side is a mistake, and the sportsbook will limit your action. On the other hand, if you bet the tough side first, it should not be difficult to find and bet the easy side afterwards.

Example of betting the tough side first.

The Dodgers are playing the Padres.

Dodgers -165 can be found at many sportsbooks. Only one place has Padres +170. The scalper should bet the Padres +170 first, because it will be easier to bet Dodgers -165 since many places have it. A scalper who bets the Dodgers -165 first might find that the Padres +170 is no longer available.

Positions after a scalp or middle

When a scalper is done placing bets, there is only one outcome: small reward, but no risk. On the other hand, when the middler is done with his bets, he can have a few different types of positions. Here are some of these different types of positions.

Closing a position: two bets with the same criteria

Scalps are usually thought of as two bets that are made almost simultaneously. But sometimes a scalper can wait to bet the second leg of the scalp. This may be due to the scalper anticipating the line will move. Or it can be due to scalping out an open wager like a future.

Example of a scalp with a game versus a future.

Initial bet: Dodgers to win the NL West

Situation: After 161 games, the Dodgers are tied with the Padres for the NL West. The two teams play each other in the last game of the season. Whoever wins game 162 wins the NL West.

Second bet: Padres to win game 162 against the Dodgers

Risk remaining: If the bet amounts are in correct proportions, the combined risk remaining is zero. The scalper has done one of the following three things: locked in a profit, locked in a loss, or locked in a push.

The initial bet and the second bet in this example are not always mirror images of each other. They are in this example because it is given that the two teams are tied for the division lead with one game to play.

Distributional spread

A distributional spread combines two bets that are related but not mirror images of each other. The two bets have different winning criteria. While some results in the final score of the game or event will have one bet as a winner and the other as a loser, there may be certain distributions of scores where both bets win or both bets lose. The typical middle is a bet with a distributional spread.

Time spread

A time spread involves two bets that partially overlap in game time. In a time spread, it is possible to win both bets, lose both bets, or win one and lose the other. This is not a middle but it is related.

Here is an example of a time spread.

Initial bet: Raiders +11 vs. Bengals in the game
Second bet: Bengals -6 in the first half vs. the Raiders

Risk remaining: In the first half of the game, you are rooting for the Bengals to cover the 6-point spread. However, you are also hoping that the Bengals do not win the first half by too many points because you still have the Raiders +11 in the game. The you would rather have the Bengals win the first half by 7 points than by 10. Once the first half ends, you are naked with the risk for the bet on the whole game. The risk in the first half of the initial bet is hedged to a degree, but the risk in the second half is not hedged.

Return on risk

When analyzing the profitability of short-term scalps and middles, it is better to use ROR (return on risk) rather than ROI (return on investment). The risk of a well-executed scalp or middle is small even though a large investment is often necessary. ROI underestimates the profitability of scalps and middles in relation to other type of bets because it is not possible to lose the entire investment.

Conclusion

Scalping and middling can be profitable activities. The scalper needs the ability to bet the same event with different lines. The middler can use the same talent as well, but the middler also needs to understand the probability distribution of games landing on certain numbers. In the modern age, scalping is difficult because books have easy access to information about the offerings of competitors.

CHAPTER 6
HEDGING

A hedge is a financial term defined as a trade that reduces the risk of a current position. Traders in the financial markets hedge their positions at times, and sports bettors hedge their bets at times too. Almost any bet can be hedged if there is enough time to make a wager and someone else willing to take the other side. But not all hedges are good ideas; some have more cost than benefit. Other hedges may exchange one risk for another without you being fairly compensated.

If lines are efficient, you theoretically are paying a vigorish to make any wager. This includes initial wagers as well as hedging wagers. Any hedge theoretically has a negative EV associated with it, just as any other wager does too. Be judicious when hedging a bet because the hedge may do more harm than good. While a hedge may reduce the risk of an existing position, if the hedge is negative EV, then the loss in EV may overshadow the reduction of risk. The question for you to ask yourself:

Is it worth paying the negative EV in a new wager in order to reduce the risk in the initial wager?

Most of the time the answer is no. Usually the negative EV in a hedge is not worth the reduction of risk in the initial wager. This includes closing a position, creating middles, hedging futures bets and most other scenarios. There are some exceptions when there are valid reasons to hedge. These reasons fall into four categories. I will describe each reason in detail and give examples in practice.

Valid Reasons to Hedge

☐   The risk of the original wager is too great

☐   The hedge has positive or zero EV

☐   The hedge was pre-planned as part of the original wager

☐   The hedge releases capital and increases the opportunity to make future positive EV bets

The risk of the original wager is too great

Sometimes the risk of a position is too great for you to stomach. The thought of losing the bet has such negative connotations that you do not mind giving up EV in order to reduce the risk. This is not usually a good situation to be in. It could mean you did not plan correctly and overbet your bankroll. You should try to bet within the limits of your bankroll as often as possible. But there are times when a wager is too good to pass up because of the high EV. Here are some examples of good initial wagers with hedging because of the size of the risk.

Example 1:

The player bets 5-team parlays on parlay cards at a local casino that is offering an amazing special of 40-1 on this weekend's parlay card. The casino is trying to attract more business and is running this incredible special for a limited number of plays. The player fills out ten different parlay cards, each with a different combination of five teams, but all with the 5th team as the New York Giants on Monday Night Football. Miraculously, every game on every parlay card for the player is a winner on Saturday and Sunday. The player realizes that if the Giants cover on Monday Night Football, he will hit a big payoff and cash every ticket. On the other hand, if the Giants do not cover, then he will not cash any tickets. Marking to market, he has theoretically won a lot of money, and that money will be lost if the Giants do not cover. If this happens, he will be extremely sad as he will have lost a great opportunity at a huge payoff. In fact, he will be so sad that it will make him sick to his stomach. The risk is simply too great for him, and a hedge is in order, even though the hedge has negative EV. The player understands he is giving up edge by hedging, but he is willing to pay the vigorish in order to reduce his risk to a level his stomach can handle.

Example 2:

An office worker enters a $100 NCAA Men's Basketball Tournament Pool. There are 200 entrants and it is a winner-take-all pool; the winner takes home a cool $20,000. On Monday morning before the finals, the office worker finds out that he is only a point behind first place. He has one of the teams in the Finals, and if his team wins, he will gain enough points to take first place. Marking to market, he has theoretically won about $10,000. Thus the risk in the final game is now $10,000 rather than the initial entry fee of $100. This risk of losing $10,000 may now be too great for the office worker to stomach losing. The best route is to seek the player in first place and try to make a fair deal with him so that they both win regardless of the winner in the Finals. Failing an agreement, the office worker may be interested in hedging and losing some EV in order to reduce this great risk. Coming away with nothing after this long ride may be too sickening to contemplate. Each person's risk preference is a personal decision.

The hedge has positive or zero EV

A hedge that has positive or zero EV is a great bet. Not only does it reduce your risk, but you are not paying to reduce the risk. Often the evaluation of the EV is subjective, so you must be able to trust your own EV calculations to determine if the hedge is actually a positive or zero EV wager. Don't fall into the trap of convincing yourself a bet is positive EV in order to justify hedging.

Example 1:

In the second example above, the office worker first decided to seek the player currently in first place to see if they could strike a fair deal. A fair deal means zero EV and is a much better alternative to hedging at a sportsbook and paying the vigorish to the casino.

Example 2:

The player bets $10 on the Pittsburgh Steelers to win Super Bowl XL at 20-1 in the beginning of the season. When the Steelers win three road playoff games to get into the Super Bowl, the player is excited to see the Steelers as a favorite against the Seattle Seahawks. At one local casino, he finds a money line on Seattle at +185. The player estimates this is a positive-EV bet. He thinks the fair line should be Seattle +180. This is a perfect and natural hedge for the player. Not only can he bet big enough to offset all of his risk on the futures bet, but he is also hedging with positive EV. He is not paying anything to reduce his risk; in fact he is being paid to do so. He can take advantage of 5 cents of positive EV as well as reduce his risk.

The hedge was pre-planned

It is possible to make a wager with a possible hedge in mind for the future. Usually these are long-shot wagers like futures and multiple-team parlays.

Without positive EV on the original wager, planning to take the negative EV of the hedge near the end of the wager would not make much sense. The negative-EV hedge needs to be small enough so it does not overshadow the positive EV on the initial wager.

Pre-planning a hedge allows you to make a bigger initial wager because you know that you have the opportunity to hedge later on, and thus your true risk is smaller than the size of your initial wager. Without the pre-planned hedge, you may not bet as large, and thus forgo positive EV. With the pre-planned hedge, you can gain more positive EV on the original wager even after discounting for the possible negative-EV hedge later on.

Here is an example of a pre-planned hedge. The player has calculated that the true odds for the New Orleans Saints to win the NFC South are 9-1 or 10%. One sportsbook is offering odds of 24-1. This is a great bet. How much should the player bet?

The player thinks about it and decides that if it came down to the final couple of weeks in the season and the Saints still have a chance to win the division, he will have tremendous risk. The player realizes he would be willing to sweat out a possible $2500 swing, but no more than that. Thus if he could not hedge, his risk appetite would allow him to bet only $100 on the Saints at 24-1, a ticket that would turn into either $0 or $2500.

But he decides he will pre-plan to hedge against the Saints in the last couple weeks of the season if they are still in the race for the division at that time, to stay within his $2500 comfort level. This pre-planned hedge allows him to bet the sportsbook's maximum of $300. It increases the positive EV and increases the risk. But the player knows that if the Saints are still in the race, he will have a chance to hedge in the last couple of weeks. The expected cost of the hedge is dwarfed by the positive EV in the original wager.

EV of initial $100 wager
    = $2400 x 10% - $100 x 90%
    = +$150
EV of initial $300 wager
    = $150 x 3
    = +$450

Now fast-forward to the last few games of the regular season. If the Saints are still in the running, the bettor is holding a ticket that soon will be worth $7500 or $0, and he'd like to reduce the swing to $2500. An easy way to do that is with a money-line wager. To demonstrate the possible cost of the pre-planned hedge, let's assume that in order to win the division, the Saints must win their last game of the year at pick 'em. The player can hedge by betting $2640 to win $2400 on the Saints to lose. That would give a combined win of $4860 or $2400, a swing he can stomach. The hedge has a negative EV of $120.

EV of pre-planned hedge
    = -$2640 x 50% + $2400 x 50%
    = -$120
Total EV of $300 wager + pre-planned hedge
    = $450 - $120
    = +$330

The combined EV of the $300 wager and the pre-planned hedge is $330, which is greater than the EV of a $100 wager ($150).

The hedge releases capital

When you own shares of stock, you do not need to put up additional capital to sell those shares. On the other hand, if you bet on one team and then decide to "sell" by betting on the other team, you usually have to come up with funds for the second bet just as you did for the first one, and you have to wait until the event is over before you can collect, even if it is a perfect scalp.

There are some betting exchanges in Europe and elsewhere where people can trade sports bets the way they trade stocks. Hedging with a slight negative EV by closing positions at these betting exchanges may be a valid reason to hedge if there is another opportunity available with greater positive EV.

Another way you could hedge and release capital is by selling your futures ticket to another bettor. Maybe you and the other bettor have a difference of opinion in the value of the futures ticket and you both think you are making a good trade.

Thoughts While Hedging

The two crucial elements in evaluating whether a hedge is worthwhile are the EV of the hedge and the risk it reduces in an initial bet that is still active. You need to balance the EV versus the change in the risk profile. Reducing risk is good, but not if the cost is too high. The right balance is based on your personal risk preferences.

Here is a 4-step thought process to evaluate the EV of the hedge and the change in the risk profile.

1. Estimate the EV of the hedge
2. Understand the risk of both the initial bet and the hedge bet
3. Evaluate the remaining risk after the hedge
4. Compare the EV to the remaining risk profile

Estimate the EV of the hedge

Estimating the EV of the hedge is crucial because it tells you how aggressive to be when hedging. You should act differently depending on whether the hedge is a positive-EV bet, a zero EV bet or a negative-EV bet. Estimating the EV of a wager may be the most difficult part of the process.

Understand the risk of the bets

Understanding the risk of any bet that you hold is always useful. Here are three issues you should figure out to assess the risk in any bet.

a. Estimate the probability of winning.

b. Calculate the current EV of the wager.

c. Determine the maximum win and maximum loss using the current EV of the wager

An understanding of these three issues for the initial wager gives you a good idea of your risk.

Here is an example. It is late in the season, and USC is in a good position to win the BCS Championship. You make that bet at 5-1 for $100. In order to win the BCS Championship, USC needs to beat UCLA in a regular season game, and then beat Ohio State in the BCS Championship game.

Estimate the probability of winning.

The fair money line on USC against UCLA is USC -450 or 81.8%. You estimate that if USC meets Ohio State, USC will be an underdog and have about a 34% chance of winning the game. Thus you expect USC has a 27.8% chance of winning the BCS Championship (81.8% x 34% = 27.8%). You have just estimated the probability of winning the initial bet.

Calculate the current EV of the wager.

You risked $100 to win $500 on the initial bet. With a current probability of 27.8% to win the bet, the current EV of the bet is:

$$= \text{(win amount x prob. of winning)}$$
$$\quad - \text{(lose amount x prob. of losing)}$$
$$= (\$500 \times 27.8\%) - (\$100 \times 72.2\%)$$
$$= +\$66.80$$

You have just calculated the current market value of the wager. You have theoretically won $66.80 on the wager.

Determine the maximum win and maximum loss

The maximum win from this point is:

$$= \text{Win amount - current market value}$$
$$= \$500 - \$66.80$$
$$= \$433.20$$

The maximum loss from this point is:

$$= \text{Loss amount - current market value}$$
$$= -\$100 - \$66.80$$
$$= -\$166.80$$

You have theoretically won $66.80 already. If you win the bet, you will win an additional $433.20 for a total of $500. If you lose the bet, then you lose the theoretical win of $66.80 plus the original risk of $100, for a total loss of $166.80.

Right now, your initial wager is equivalent to a wager of $166.80 to win $433.20 with $66.80 in your theoretical account. The perfect hedge with zero EV is to bet $433.20 to win $166.80 that USC will not win the BCS Championship. With that hedge, there would be no risk and a profit of $66.80 would be locked in.

Notice that the EV calculation using the current market value shows an EV of 0. This shows that the wager has been marked to your estimated value.

$$(\$433.20 \times 27.8\%) - (\$166.80 \times 72.2\%) = \$0$$

Evaluate the risk after the hedge

If you hedge your initial bet perfectly, you will have zero risk remaining. An example was shown in the previous section. Other times you can hedge with a wager that is not exactly the same as the mirror image of the original wager, but is close. The combination of the initial bet and the hedge may have a smaller risk, but there will still be risk remaining. The risk remaining could result in a bigger potential loss in the worst case scenario than without the hedge. You should understand what the new risk will be before betting the hedge.

Here is an example of analyzing the risk remaining after a hedge.

Let's say you bet Oklahoma -1.5 against Texas, risking $110 to win $100. You think the fair value should be Oklahoma -3 and you think you have positive EV in your initial bet.

On the day of the game, the line in the game moves to Oklahoma -3. Since you think the fair value should be Oklahoma -3, you decide there is no valid reason to hedge in taking Texas +3 -110. You are comfortable with the risk and see no need to make a negative-EV hedge. If the line had moved to Texas +3.5 -110, then you would find that to be slightly positive EV and you would be happy to bet that as a hedge.

As you search for prices in many Las Vegas sportsbooks, you find another bet that is a closely related to your original bet. The bet has positive EV and is also a hedge to your initial wager, although not a perfect hedge. The bet is the money line on Texas at +160. Based on a fair line of Texas +3, you are confident that the money line on Texas at +160 is a fantastic bet. Not only is it a positive-EV bet, but it also hedges your original bet of Oklahoma -1.5. The risk remaining from these two bets combined is if Oklahoma wins by exactly 1 point, you will lose both bets. These two bets combined is a positive-EV reverse-middle.

Given the positive EV, the Texas money line is a good bet and also hedges your risk in the Oklahoma -1.5 initial bet. The risk remaining (if Oklahoma wins by exactly 1) is a scenario that is a bigger loss than the worst case scenario before the hedge. But you are comfortable with the fact you may lose both bets in that scenario, given the positive EV of both bets.

This example is just one possible risk profile of two combined bets. Chapter 5 contains descriptions of some other general risk profiles that can occur with a combination of wagers.

Compare the EV to the risk profile

The last step is to compare the EV to the remaining risk of the combined bets and use that information to help evaluate if there is a valid reason to hedge. As mentioned earlier in this chapter, most of the time the negative EV in the hedge is not worth the risk reduction of the initial bet. It is up to you to evaluate your own risk preferences and to make sure you have a valid reason to hedge.

Table 2 shows whether a hedge is worthwhile depending on the EV of the hedge and its risk reduction on existing bets.

The remaining risk can be larger than the initial risk if the hedge has a low correlation with the mirror image of the initial bet. If the EV of the hedge is positive, then this may be acceptable to you. But if the EV of the hedge is zero or negative, then it is not acceptable and you should pass on the hedge.

When the hedge has positive EV, it is usually a no-brainer to make the bet. The only time it is unclear is if it increases the risk profile, in which case it is not truly a hedge.

When the hedge has zero or neutral EV, it is a no-brainer to hedge if it reduces risk. But if the risk is either unchanged or increased with a zero EV hedge, then it is better to pass on it.

Table 2
Analysis of Hedges

EV of Hedge	Change in Risk	Action to Take
Positive EV	Reduced	Hedge
Positive EV	Unchanged	Hedge
Positive EV	Increased	Unclear
Zero EV	Reduced	Hedge
Zero EV	Unchanged	Pass
Zero EV	Increased	Pass
Negative EV	Reduced	Unclear
Negative EV	Unchanged	Pass
Negative EV	Increased	Pass

When the hedge has negative EV, the only time you should even think about betting the hedge is if it reduces the risk of existing bets. Then you should make sure there is a valid reason to hedge.

Sportsbooks Hedge Too

When lines move at a sportsbook, it can be due to new information such as injuries and weather or copying line moves at other sportsbooks. But line moves are often based on action, meaning that the sportsbook has had enough bets on one side and no longer want any more exposure on that same side. To encourage other bettors to bet the other side so the sportsbook can balance their risk better, the sportsbook moves the line. The line move could be a change in the point spread or a move in the money line of the point spread. A sportsbook moving a line based on action is a form of hedging. The book moves a line to encourage bettors to bet the other side and thus hedge the book's risk. Here are two examples of line moves:

Original Line:
    Dallas -5 -110
    Atlanta +5 -110

One way to move the line if customers are betting heavily on Dallas -5:

Dallas -5.5 -110
Atlanta +5.5 -110

A second way to move the line:

Dallas -5 -120
Atlanta +5 +100

A sportsbook that moves the line to Dallas -5.5 is taking the risk of being middled. A worst-case scenario for the sportsbook is if Dallas wins by exactly 5, because the book is putting itself at risk to lose to customers who bet Atlanta +5.5, and push against the customers who bet Dallas -5. If the sportsbook manages its lines well, then it is likely being paid enough vigorish on both sides to warrant this risk.

When a sportsbook moves the money line on the point spread and keeps the point spread the same, as in the second example, it does not put itself at the risk of being middled. Square customers are used to betting lines at -110. When they encounter a line of -120, they may think the sportsbook is trying to take advantage of them. This is an erroneous thought because customers can take Atlanta +5 +100 if they wanted to, but some square customers do think this way. It is possible moving the money line on the point spread will scare off this type of customer, and it is this type of customer the sportsbook wants to keep most. So moving the point spread rather than the money line may make the most business sense depending on the sportsbook's customer base.

Conclusion

Hedging is overrated and overused. Sports bettors as a group hedge too often. Even professional financial traders on Wall Street hedge too often. There is a natural human tendency to lock in a profit and reduce risk; unfortunately it is often at the expense of EV. As the saying goes, a bird in the hand is better than two in the bush. But two in the bush is better than a bird in the hand if there is a greater than 50% chance you can catch each bird in the bush. This is the way a sharp sports bettor should think.

Not all hedges are bad decisions. There are times when hedging is correct. In the first part of this chapter, I showed the valid reasons to hedge. In the latter part of this chapter, I showed what to think about when hedging. In the next chapter, I will show some common mistakes made when hedging. Using these guidelines, you will be able to proceed more intelligently when considering hedging.

CHAPTER 7
HEDGE
MISTAKES

If there are no valid reasons to hedge, then it is a mistake to hedge. Most bettors do not have valid reasons when they hedge; here are some of their possible mistakes.

Hedging After Line Movement

A common mistake sports bettors make is hedging their bets when the line moves in their favor without regard to whether the hedge is positive EV or negative EV. For example, you bet on a team -3 points and then the line moves to -5 before the game starts, with no new information such as injuries or a changing weather forecast. Some bettors will now bet on the other team at +5 as a hedge and create the possibility of winning both bets. This knee-jerk reaction gets you into a seemingly nice middle opportunity, but it may not be worth it if the hedge is a negative-EV bet. You are probably better off not hedging, and keeping the risk in the initial bet. The issue that confuses some bettors is that the combination of the initial bet and the hedge is positive EV. But since the hedge is a negative-EV bet, it means the positive EV on the initial bet is greater than the positive EV on the combination of the initial bet and the hedge.

Here is an example. In a small sportsbook, you bet $100 on over 199 on a NBA game. You trust your handicapping which shows the right number to be 203. If you had the opportunity, you would have been happy to bet $500 on the over, but this sportsbook's limit is $100 on NBA totals.

As the time gets closer to tip-off, the line starts to creep up, and five minutes prior to tip-off, the total has moved up to 202. Betting under 202 as a hedge is a mistake in this case, more so if you have to pay the vigorish. You believe the number should be 203, so taking under 202 is a negative-EV bet. It is a mistake to bet under 202 just because you have over 199 and the line moved in your favor. Even if you had bet your preferred amount of $500, there is no valid reason to hedge. Although the combination of over 199 and under 202 has positive EV, the lone bet of over 199 has greater EV.

If the total had moved to 203, hedging is still a mistake if you have to pay the vigorish to bet it. If the line moves to 203.5 -110, then hedging may be worthwhile depending on what you think of the value of the half point from 203 to 203.5. If you think the half point is worth exactly 10 cents, then the under would be a zero EV bet and it would be right to take it as a hedge.

Avoiding a Reverse Middle

In the previous section, the mistake was making a negative-EV bet as a hedge when the line moves. Avoiding a positive-EV hedge because it creates a reverse middle is the opposite mistake. Bettors who make this mistake are worried about the small possibility of losing both the initial bet and the hedge. In the previous section, the mistake is paying too much to get into a middle opportunity. In this section, the mistake is giving up a positive-EV opportunity to avoid a possible reverse middle. Here is an example:

Initial bet: Philadelphia Eagles -5.5 -110 vs. Green Bay Packers

You have handicapped this game and think the fair line is Philadelphia -7, and thus you think there is positive EV in taking Philadelphia -5.5 -110.

Later in the week, there is news that Donovan McNabb has injured his throwing hand in practice and is out for the rest of the year. You reevaluate the Eagles without McNabb and now handicap the fair line as Philadelphia -2.5. The line has not moved down as much, and you have the opportunity to make this positive-EV bet that is also a hedge:

Possible positive-EV hedge: Green Bay +3.5 -110 vs. Philadelphia Eagles.

You think the fair line is Philadelphia -2.5. That means a bet of Green Bay +3.5 -110 has positive EV. Even though making this bet would put you into a possible reverse middle when combined with the original bet of Eagles -5.5, you should still make the bet because it is a positive-EV bet. If you had not made the initial bet, you would have been happy to bet Green Bay +3.5. You should be happy to make that bet even though you have made the other bet.

Unfortunately, some bettors will avoid this positive-EV hedge because they are scared of creating a reverse middle and losing both sides. This can happen: If the Eagles win by exactly 4 or 5 points, both bets will lose. But given the handicapped numbers that you generated, you should be making the bet because the EV is great relative to the risk of being middled. It is possible that the risk of being middled is too great in some situations, but it is important to analyze those risks and compare them to the EV rather than avoiding them just because of the possibility of a reverse middle.

Increasing Risk with a Hedge

A correlation of zero means the two bets are not related; winning one wager gives no information about how likely the other wager is to win. Looking to hedge means looking for a bet negatively correlated to your initial wager. If there is close to zero correlation, then there is no hedge, and the bet is evaluated just like any other independent bet.

Hedging a Lost Cause

Bettors will sometimes try to recoup the money they expect to lose in a wager that now has a low probability of winning. They think about making a second bet and rationalize it as a hedge when in fact it is not. If an initial bet has a low chance of winning, you do not have much risk in the bet anymore; the value is already lost. It is a mistake to chase good money after lost money, especially if the good money is being bet on a negative-EV wager.

Example 1

You bet the Boston Celtics to win the Atlantic Division. With 20 games to go, they are 15 games out of first place. Your bet has a tiny chance of winning, which means there is little exposure left in your original wager. To bet against the Boston Celtics as a hedge in any individual game does not make sense. Those bets on individual games against the Celtics do not hedge the initial bet. Some bettors will rationalize betting against the Celtics as a way to recoup the money they lost on the Celtics to win the division.

Example 2

Other times, bettors make the mistake of hedging a bet that has a high chance of winning by betting too much on the hedge. Hedging may not be a bad idea, especially if it is a zero EV or positive-EV bet, but hedging too much on a zero EV or negative-EV bet will increase risk unnecessarily.

You bet $10 on the Orlando Magic to win the Atlantic Division at 8 to 1 odds. With 10 games to go, Orlando is up by 6 games and you estimate the team has a 95% chance of winning the division. If Orlando loses its next game, its chances will decrease to 92%.

EV of the division ticket before tonight's game:
95% x $90 = $85.50

EV of the division bet if Orlando loses tonight's game
92% x $90 = $82.80

If Orlando loses tonight's game, the EV of your division ticket will go down by $2.70 ($85.50 - $82.80).

Betting more than $2.70 as a hedge is over-hedging and is a mistake, especially if the hedge is a negative-EV bet.

Hedging the Last Leg of a Parlay

This mistake is not necessarily in the hedge, but in the original parlay. Some bettors like to hedge the last leg of a parlay if they are lucky to have won all the first legs. Before the last leg of the parlay, they realize they can lock in a profit and they cannot resist.

Instead of paying the vigorish to bet against the last team of the parlay, you should simply play a parlay with fewer teams. For example, instead of playing a 5-team parlay where you know you are going to hedge if you win the first four games, you should simply play a 4-team parlay instead.

The exception to this is if the sportsbook is offering better relative odds for choosing more teams in a parlay. In that case, you may have decided ahead of time to hedge and calculated the cost of the hedge into the parlay. That is an exception though and is not usually the case.

This mistake is made when players have the lottery mentality. They want to hit it big and get a lot of bang for their buck. These players will tend to play parlays with many teams so they can win big if they get really lucky. However if they do get lucky and have just one or two teams to go to win the parlay, often they get nervous with their newfound risk of losing the parlay now that it has tremendous value. Hedging is not necessarily a mistake if they feel the risk is too high and cannot stomach losing. The mistake was putting themselves in that position in the first place by playing too many teams in the parlay.

Hedging the Second Half

Some bettors will look to hedge their full-game bets at halftime if they can get into a middle situation. Usually the second-half bet is a negative-EV bet if the sportsbook is doing its job profitably. And usually you have no valid reason to hedge. Of course, if the second-half bet is a positive or zero EV bet, then it is a good idea to hedge. Here is an example of a second-half hedge bet that is a mistake.

You took the Giants +3.5 versus the Eagles. At halftime the Giants are up 14-0. The second-half line is the Eagles -4. Many will bet the Eagles -4 in the second half as a hedge against their bets on the game. The thought process is to create a big middle. You will win both bets (or tie one side and win the other) if the Giants win by 1 through 10 points or if the Eagles win by 1 through 3 points. This big middle is enticing. However, you already have a high chance of winning the initial wager. The benefit of the big middle did not come about from the second-half bet, but rather from the increased EV of the initial wager based on the points scored in the first half.

In football and basketball, second-half bets are popular. You can sometimes take advantage of the expectation of which side other players will bet in the second-half. To do it requires that you understand which team the money was bet on before the game, line movement, the type of bettors who moved the line, the type of customers who frequent that sportsbook, and the risk profile of the sportsbook. There is a small window of time when the second-half bet is available; that can mean more diversity of lines between sportsbooks than you typically see for game lines. There is considerable movement of lines for second-half bets due to a high volume of bets in a short time period.

If you know other bettors will hedge their bets and play a specific side in the second half, you may be able to use that information by betting that side when the second-half line is first posted and get the opening number before the sportsbook starts to move the lines due to action. After the line moves due to the flood of other bettors betting that side, you can come in and bet the other side to create a nice scalp or middle opportunity. Depending on the situation, a better alternative may be to just make that second bet after the line moves.

Missing a Bet

Some bettors know that hedging is generally a bad idea, so they never consider the idea of hedging. This can be a mistake because it may mean passing up opportunities to make more money. Planning a future hedge can allow you to make larger initial positive-EV bets. In order to justify the planned hedge, the combination of the positive EV in the larger initial bet and the negative EV of the planned hedge must be greater than the positive EV in the alternative smaller initial wager.

One situation where planning a future hedge is useful is when you think there is a high chance the line will move so much that you can bet the other side at a better price at a later time. This means you can make an initial bet that you would not normally make (or a larger than normal initial bet) because you know you are going to hedge it in the future and probably have a nice scalp or middle.

Without the possibility of hedging, you may not make the initial bet at all and miss out on making some money.

Here is an example where the line has a high chance of increasing. One bettor completely ignores the thought of hedging, while the other bettor takes advantage of a planned hedge.

It is Tuesday night and the Dodgers are playing the Giants. Before the game starts, several sportsbooks already have lines on the Wednesday game, which is set at Dodgers -160, Giants +150. That seems like a fair line.

In the first inning of the Tuesday game, Barry Bonds pulls a hamstring muscle while chasing a fly in left field. He is taken out of the game after the play and later the broadcaster announces that Bonds will be put on the Disabled List. This means he will definitely not play in Wednesday's game. Bonds is still one of the best hitters in baseball, and having him out of the lineup is a big blow to the Giants. The Wednesday line of Dodgers -160 is now a great bet without Bonds in the Giants lineup.

Bettor #1 is a smart player who tries to take advantage of mistakes made by sportsbooks. But he does not think hedging is a good idea since he is willing to take any risks that he bets on and is not happy with making any negative-EV bets. When he sees the injury to Bonds, he quickly races to the sportsbook and makes a normal sized bet. The line is still Dodgers -160 and he bets $160 to win $100. In the morning, he notices the line has moved up to Dodgers -200, Giants +180. He is happy with his nice positive-EV bet on the Dodgers -160. He does not hedge because he is not interested in making a negative-EV bet to get out of his risk. Given the size of his original wager, it is smart of him not to hedge. The fair value on the Dodgers is -190 (or 65.5%), and the EV of his initial bet is:

Bettor #1's EV: $100 x 65.5% - $160 x 34.5% = +$10.30

Bettor #2 is also a smart player who tries to take advantage of mistakes made by sportsbooks. But he is willing to keep an open mind and tries to make as much money as possible. His normal sized bet is the same as Bettor #1, but instead of betting $160 to win $100 on the Dodgers when he sees the injury to Bonds, he bets three times as big, $480 to win $300. In the morning when the Bonds injury is embedded in the new line, Bettor #2 happily makes a negative-EV bet by betting $200 on the Giants at +180, thus scalping out two-thirds of his original wager. He is left with a net position of $120 to win $100 on the Dodgers, which is superior to Bettor #1's $160 to win $100. Here is the combined EV of Bettor #2's bets:

Bettor #2's normal sized bet on the Dodgers -160:
$100 x 65.5% - $160 x 34.5% = +$10.30
Bettor #2's extra $200 that he plans to hedge:
$200 x 65.5% - $320 x 34.5% = $20.60
Bettor #2's hedge bet on the Giants at +180:
$360 x 34.5% - $200 x 65.5% = -$6.80
Total EV: $10.30 + $20.60 - $6.80 = +$24.10

Bettor #2 is well aware that the hedge is a negative-EV bet. However, he also knows that without the hedge, he would not have made the initial bet of $480 to win $300. If he was not going to hedge, he would simply make his normal sized bet of $160 to win $100. He has counted on making a negative-EV hedge in the future in order to increase his overall EV. In the end, Bettor #2 has $13.80 more EV than Bettor #1.

Bettor #2 did take some additional risk. There is no guarantee the line would go in the direction that he hoped. The line might have stayed unchanged or might have moved in the other direction.

CHAPTER 8 NFL SEASON WINS

NFL regular season win (RSW) totals are popular bets and commonly available at many sportsbooks before the start of the season. You can bet for or against a team by taking the over or the under. In other futures lines, such as who will win the Super Bowl, the high vigorish that most sportsbooks build into their lines makes it tough to find any justifiable wagers. You can bet on a team to win the Super Bowl in those lines; but you cannot bet against a particular team to win the Super Bowl. Many sportsbooks take advantage of this and offer odds on the 32 NFL teams that add up to greater than 150%. Some sportsbooks have the gall to offer cumulative lines in excess of 200%! In that environment, it is tough to find any worthwhile wagers.

For RSW totals, sportsbooks are willing to take bets on both sides. You can bet on a team either to win more games than expected or to win fewer games than expected. Since you can bet on either side, the sportsbooks must offer relatively fair lines so they have balanced action. These fairer lines give smart bettors a chance to find some positive-EV wagers.

This chapter presumes you have already made your own analysis on the relative strength of each team. But that alone is not enough to find positive-EV bets in RSW totals. The following skills are also needed to exploit inefficiencies in the RSW total markets, and they are discussed throughout this chapter.

☐ Projecting lines for games in the future

☐ Understanding how the football betting market works

☐ Understanding the risk, rewards and opportunity costs of long-term wagers

☐ Understanding how to compare and contrast one line to another to find the best value

Sum of Wins is at Most 256

There are 32 teams in the NFL and they each play 16 games. This means there can be no more than 256 wins spread among the 32 teams. $(32 \times 16 / 2 = 256)$

Although rare, ties sometimes do happen in the NFL. A tie is not a win with regards to the RSW wager, nor is it considered a half-win. For the purposes of RSW totals, a tie is the same as a loss. Thus it is possible for the total number of wins for all teams combined to be lower than 256 if there are one or more ties during the season.

A maximum of 256 wins during the season is a simple fact, but it is still an important one to consider. Most sportsbooks shade their NFL RSW totals toward the high side. This is probably because most bettors like betting on a team rather than against. Tourists, for example, are more likely to bet on their favorite teams to go over the total. The sportsbooks are expecting more bets on the over than the under, and they shade their lines accordingly.

While in Las Vegas in early August 2006, I added up the total number of wins from one of the major sportsbooks. The lines were typical of lines at other sportsbooks. The RSW totals at this sportsbook added up to 262 - six more than the 256 maximum. Caution: Blindly betting all the unders does not have positive EV due to the vigorish that the sportsbook charges. On average, you lay -115 to bet the over and -115 to bet the under (a 30 cent margin). Although you cannot blindly bet the under profitably, the fact that the sum of the wins adds up to 262 means that if there are positive-EV bets to be found in RSW totals, they are more likely to be on the under than the over.

Rate Each Game

A good step in evaluating RSW totals is to assign a game line to each game for each team. Do not do it for any single team alone; do it for the whole league. Stay within the guidelines of 256 wins for the entire league. If you assign the Patriots a 75% chance of beating the Bills, you should assign the Bills a 25% chance of beating the Patriots in the same game. If you are more comfortable with point spread lines, then project those first and then convert them into money lines or win percentages.

Some bettors make the mistake of assigning a straight win or loss in a particular game solely based on the expectation that the team will be a favorite or underdog. Reporters, commentators and analysts in the media often make this mistake. Certainties and absolutes do not exist in the NFL. Instead, you should be dealing with probabilities. A team that is expected to be the favorite in every game is not expected to go 16-0 for the season.

Strength of Schedule

The strength of schedule should be built into the expected line you project for each team and each game. For example, you may notice that some good teams are not projected to have great win-loss records because they have a tough schedule coming up. On the other hand, some average teams may be expected to have decent win-loss records because they play soft schedules. Projecting individual lines for each game based on the opponents takes the strength of schedule into effect. Over a 16-game season, quality of opponents can matter a lot.

Compare to Posted Lines

A good way to check your work is to compare the lines you projected with the NFL Games of the Year lines put out by some sportsbooks before the season starts.

Las Vegas casinos such as the Las Vegas Hilton and the Palms have been offering NFL Games of the Year, but with lower limits than on current games. The lines have information value. If the books' lines do not match closely with the lines you made, then you should take a closer look at your own lines. You may be inspired to make some adjustments. Or, if you still agree with your original work, you may have found solid bets on individual Games of the Year.

For example, if a sportsbook has the line for Miami at New England as Patriots -7, but you are expecting Patriots -4, then you should think about making adjustments to your projections and/or betting the Dolphins +7 for that particular game.

2006

Table 3 is the projection I made in August 2006 for the 2006 Carolina Panthers. I used a power rating system where I valued each team based on how I thought it would fare against a .500 team on a neutral field. Then I added 8% to the home team's

Table 3
2006 Carolina Panthers RSW Projection

Week	Opponent	Win %	Point spread	
1	ATL	0.67	-4.5	
2	at MIN	0.585	-3	-102
3	at TB	0.51	0	
4	NO	0.76	-7.5	
5	CLE	0.76	-7.5	
6	at BAL	0.525	-1	
7	at CIN	0.475	+1	
8	DAL	0.595	-3	-106
9	BYE			
10	TB	0.67	-4.5	
11	STL	0.785	-8.5	
12	at WAS	0.465	+2.5	
13	at PHI	0.495	0	
14	NYG	0.64	-4	
15	PIT	0.575	-3	+102
16	at ATL	0.51	0	
17	at NO	0.6	-3	-108
	Total	9.62		

chances of winning and subtracted 8% from the visiting team's chances of winning. These projections on the Panthers were not done in isolation; they were done along with projections for the other 31 NFL teams to avoid inconsistency in any particular match-up. Note that for games lined at 3, I also include a money line since not all games lined at 3 are equal.

The next step was to compare my lines to some sportsbooks' Games of the Year lines. If my lines were hugely different from their lines, then I knew I had to make an adjustment to my numbers or make a wager on one of the Games of the Year. I also took into account the time value of money and the risk of the sportsbook when making this decision.

Many sportsbooks already had lines for Week 1 of the NFL regular season. The line for the CAR vs ATL game looked to be CAR -4.5 as of early August. My number for the first game of the season agreed with the market's number.

The Las Vegas Hilton does a solid job of setting lines for the Games of the Year. Here are lines they had on the board on August 1 involving the Panthers. My line is in parenthesis.

Week 2: CAR -3 at MIN (-3 -102)
Week 6: CAR +1 at BAL (-1)
Week 7: CAR +1.5 at CIN (+1)
Week 8: CAR -3.5 vs DAL (-3 -106)
Week 10: CAR -5.5 vs TB (-4.5)
Week 13: CAR -1 at PHI (0)

The lines at the Hilton matched my projections closely. The differences in the games against BAL, CIN, TB and PHI were not important because they were over "dead" numbers that occur in-frequently in the NFL (0, 1 and 5). The differences in those four games also offset each other, so I did not need to worry that I was consistently overvaluing or undervaluing the Panthers relative to the Hilton's lines.

The biggest difference was the game against DAL. I had CAR -3 -106 while the Hilton had CAR -3.5. The half point from 3 to 3.5 is the largest half point in the NFL. About 10% of all games where the home team is a 3 to 3.5 point favorite are actually won by the home team by exactly 3 points. That reflects about a 23 cent dif-ference between CAR -3 and CAR -3.5. My projection of CAR

-3 -106 is equivalent to CAR -3.5 +117 or DAL +3.5 -117. I could bet DAL +3.5 -110 at the Hilton, so against my numbers, there was 7 cents of edge in betting the DAL side.

This meant I was underrating CAR relative to the Hilton's line in this particular game. I had to decide whether I wanted to make any adjustments to my power ratings for CAR and/or DAL based on this difference, or wager on DAL +3.5 -110, or do nothing at all. I decided to do nothing as I was comfortable with my numbers and not thrilled about only 7 cents of edge on a bet that would take more than two months to resolve.

The Wavy-Ruler Effect

Projecting game lines for 16 games is not easy. Who knows what teams will look like by December? In August 2005, few thought the Eagles would be such a bad team by December. Then again, few thought that they would be playing without both Donovan McNabb and Terrell Owens. If you are not comfortable with this uncertainty, it may be best to avoid RSW totals and other long-term wagers.

Imagine holding a ruler horizontally. Wave it up and down. The part by your fingertips moves a little; the other end moves much more. This is a good analogy for projecting football lines for a team over an entire season. The points on the ruler close to your finger have some variability, but not much. The points on the other end have much greater variability. Although the farther points have greater variability, the center of the wave for them is the same as for the points closer to your fingers. You are expecting greater variability in the lines of the latter weeks of the season, but that variability will be around your original expectation. If your projections are good, then you may expect something like this in Week 1 vs. Week 16:

Week 1: you project DAL Even Money
Expected variability with 80% confidence interval: DAL +2.5 to DAL -2.5, with the midpoint around DAL pick 'em.

Week 16: you project DAL Even Money
Expected variability with 80% confidence interval: DAL +7 to DAL -7, with the midpoint around DAL pick 'em.

In both Week 1 and Week 16, you expected the midpoint to be DAL pick 'em. However, you expect greater variability in Week 16 than Week 1. In general, if you have a good midpoint, the variability can help you or it could hurt you, with equal chance; it does not increase or decrease the EV of your wager.

Other Considerations

The time value of money, opportunity costs and sportsbook risk are concerns for any futures wagers, including RSW totals.

Time value of money

You are giving the sportsbook the money in August, and you will not get paid until late December or early January. Instead of making the wager, you could have placed the money in an interest-bearing account or another investment.

Opportunity cost

During the season you may find an opportunity to make a positive-EV wager for a large amount of money, but be illiquid due to much of your funds being tied up in futures bets. If that happens, the futures bets have cost you money.

Sportsbook risk

Sportsbook risk is also important to consider. How sure are you that you will get paid in late December or early January when your wager is a winner? In Nevada, the risk is negligible. The risk can be greater outside of Nevada.

Value of a Half Win

Sometimes different sportsbooks have different totals for the same team. One sportsbook may have the total at 9, while another has the total at 9.5. The vigorish attached to the over and under compensates for the difference in the total. Compare the money lines for the different totals to see which is the better wager.

As a rule of thumb, the probability that an NFL team wins the same number of games as its total (assuming it is a whole number) is about 20%. See chapter 11 in Stanford Wong's *Sharp Sports Betting* for more information on this topic.

As an example of the 20% rule of thumb, if the total on the Chicago Bears RSW is 9, then the Bears have about a 20% chance of winning exactly 9 games. Thus the Bears are expected to win more than 9 games 40% of the time and fewer than 9 games 40% of the time.

Bears Wins	Probability
More than 9	40%
Exactly 9	20%
Less than 9	40%

Those numbers can be used to value totals of 9.5, 9 and 8.5. With a total of 9.5, under 9.5 includes both percentages in "Exactly 9" and "Less than 9"; under 9.5 equals 60% (20% + 40%). With a total of 8.5, over 8.5 includes both percentages in "Exactly 9" and "More than 9"; over 8.5 equals 60% (20% + 40%).

With a total of 9, if the Bears win exactly 9 games, then all bets are refunded. Thus when considering over 9 or under 9, the important percentages are "More than 9" and "Less than 9." Each has a 40% chance, so they are equally likely to happen; each wager has a 50% chance of winning or losing when the pushes are not considered. It is useful to think this way because all wagers are expressed in terms of the money line.

Here is the formula when ties are refunded. Then convert this percentage into a money line to see if the line put up by the sportsbook has value.

% Over X wins
    = % More than X wins / (Total % without pushes)

In the case of the Bears:

% Over 9 wins
    = % More than 9 wins / (Total % without pushes)
    = 40% / (40% + 40%)
    = 50%
    = +100 in the money line

Below is a summary of the probabilities and the equivalent money line for the Bears.

Wager	Prob	Money Line
Over 9.5	40%	150
Under 9.5	60%	-150
Over 9	50%	100
Under 9	50%	100
Over 8.5	60%	-150
Under 8.5	40%	150

When the line is around even money (50%), a 10% change is worth about 50 cents in the money line. This can be seen in the table above by comparing over 9.5 to over 9 and over 9 to over 8.5. This relationship breaks down a bit when the initial probability is not 50%, but it is still a useful rule of thumb to use for RSW wagers.

Here is an example. You want to bet the under in the Bengals RSW. Which of these two wagers has better value?

Cincinnati under 9.5 -130
Cincinnati under 9 +100

Adding 50 cents to under 9.5 -130 shows that it is equal to under 9 +120. Therefore, under 9.5 -130 is superior to under 9 +100.

Spreadsheet

SharpSportsBetting.com has a spreadsheet available under the link "Prop Tools" that is useful in calculating the value of a half-win in all sports. (The spreadsheet makes the assumption that every game has an equal chance of being won. If the expected number of wins for a team is 4 out of 16 games, then the team is assumed to have a 25% chance of winning each game.)

Value of the Vig

Once you have an expectation for the number of wins, you must compare it to the line and the amount you have to lay. Not all lines are at even money, so you must be able to value the vigorish relative to the total and the expected wins you projected. For example, if you expect a team to win 9.62 games, is it worthwhile to bet under 10 -120? You need a mechanism to answer this question. Using a computer to make calculations is advised. But in Las Vegas sportsbooks, you often find yourself having to make an estimate on the fly without a computer handy. Having a rule of thumb can be helpful in those cases.

The rule of thumb is similar to that for the value of the half win.

0.01 wins is equal to 1 cent in the money line
0.1 wins is equal to 10 cents in the money line
0.5 wins is equal to 50 cents in the money line

Here is an example. You expect a team to win 8.36 games. You can bet under 9 -130. Is this a good bet?

Using the rule of thumb, under 9 is worth -164.

Work shown: 9 wins (the line) minus 8.36 (the expected number of wins) equal 0.64 wins. Using the rule of thumb, 0.64 wins

Table 4
2006 NFL Season-Wins Picks

Team	Neutral	Exp	Rule of Thumb	Bet	EV
CAR	9.92	9.62	Under 10 -138	Under 10 Even	38 cents
CIN	9.04	8.36	Under 9 -164	Under 9 -130	34 cents
DEN	9.84	9.63	Under 10 -137	Under 10 -105	32 cents
NYG	8.96	8.33	Under 9 -167	Under 9 -135	32 cents
PIT	10.00	9.61	Under 10 -139	Under 10 -105	34 cents
WAS	9.20	8.86	Under 9 -114	Under 9 +120	34 cents

Key:

"Neutral" is my estimate of expected wins for a team if it faced .500 teams on neutral fields in all 16 games.

"Exp" is my expected wins for each team given its 2006 schedule.

"Rule of Thumb" reflects the fair vigorish given the numbers in the Actual column.

"Bet" is the wager I made while in Las Vegas.

"EV" is my estimated edge, expressed in cents.

converts to 64 cents in the money line. If the expected number of wins is exactly 9, then under 9 is worth +100 or -100. With 8.36 expected wins, under 9 wins is a favorite. Take -100 and "add" -64 cents to get -164. Under 9 -164 is the fair value line given 8.36 expected wins. The line is under 9 -130, but you think it is worth -164. So you think there is a positive EV of 34 cents in betting under 9 -130.

The rule of thumb is a shortcut, and becomes less accurate as the money line gets farther away from even money.

My RSW Picks for 2006

Table 4 shows six bets I made in August 2006 for the coming NFL season. These plays were published in the *Two Plus Two Internet Magazine* on September 1, 2006.

These six wagers have the following in common:

☐ The total is 9 or greater in all of them. I found value in the under in all of them.

☐ They all made the playoffs in 2005; three were division winners and three were wild-card teams

☐ The expected wins for each team is less than what its expected wins would have been had it played a neutral schedule. This is due to each of those teams playing a tough schedule.

All the teams on my list made the playoffs in 2005. The bookmakers project them all to be successful again in 2006. I projected that if they played neutral schedules, they would average 9.49 wins.

Table 5
2006 NFL Season-Wins Picks: Recap

Team	Exp	Bet	Wins	Result
CAR	9.62	Under 10 Even	8	Win
CIN	8.36	Under 9 -130	8	Win
DEN	9.63	Under 10 -105	9	Win
NYG	8.33	Under 9 -135	8	Win
PIT	9.61	Under 10 -105	8	Win
WAS	8.86	Under 9 +120	5	Win

With three teams lined at 10 wins and three teams lined at 9 wins, it looks at first glance like I am agreeing with the bookmakers. The difference is due to the tough schedules that these teams play. My projections reduce their expected wins from an average of 9.49 with a neutral schedule to 9.07 with their 2006 schedules. That difference of 0.42 wins explains why I found positive EV in these bets.

The results turned out to be good for all six under bets. All six teams won fewer games than the over/under line. All six teams also won fewer games than I expected. This shows that good luck was also involved in winning all six bets. Table 5 shows the actual wins by these teams in 2006.

Conclusion

You can find positive EV in NFL RSW totals. You are aided by the two-sided lines maintained by the sportsbooks, unlike other types of futures bets. In this chapter, I have shown some issues to consider when analyzing these wagers, as well as the risks and opportunity costs associated with long-term bets. Examples of bets I made before the 2006 NFL season and their results were also shown to help describe the thought process.

CHAPTER 9
NFL PARLAY
CARDS

Many sportsbooks in Nevada offer parlay cards. These are cards with preset lines for the weekend's football games, and listed parlay odds for different numbers of teams picked.

Lines on the board may move, but lines on the parlay cards do not change. If a line moves a lot, the sportsbook eliminates that game from use on a parlay card.

The odds on the parlay cards are set to the advantage of the sportsbook. It is usually a nice profit center in the sportsbook due to the horrible odds offered. But square players still like them because of the lottery mentality of a possible big payoff. Even with the bad odds, there are still some possible positive EV situations.

Parlay cards come in different variations. Casinos offer parlay cards that differ in lines, odds and rules. Be careful in checking all of these issues, which are printed on the back of the card.

I will use an example of a 3-team parlay that pays 6.5 for 1 throughout this section. With a few adjustments, you should be able to calculate the numbers for any other variation using this section as a guide.

The payoff offered for 3-team parlays is usually no better than 6.5 for 1. Often the odds are worse, but let's use an optimistic example. If you win, the casino will give you $6.50 for every $1 that you bet. This is different than the way sportsbooks state their odds for most other bets. $1 out of the $6.50 is the amount you paid to make the wager. In other words, a 6.5 for 1 payoff really means odds of 5.5 to 1. This can be misleading and many square bettors fall for it without realizing it.

Break-Even Rates

First convert the odds into a break-even winning percentage. 6.5 for 1 converts to a break-even winning percentage of 15.4% (1/6.5).

Second, convert this break-even winning percentage to an equivalent winning percentage on the three games. Since there are three teams, take the cube root of 15.4%. This is not as scary as it sounds; the formula in Excel is =(1/6.5)^(1/3). The answer is 53.6%.

You need to be able to win each game at the rate of 53.6% in order to break even to the odds on the parlay card. This is higher than the 52.4% break-even rate on straight bets at -110 juice.

This process can be used to evaluate the equivalent break-even winning percentage for parlays with more teams too. Here is an example of a 4-team parlay that pays 11 for 1.

The break-even winning percentage for a 4-team parlay paying 11 for 1 is 9.09% (1/11). Next, find the equivalent winning percentage on the four games. Take 9.09% to the (1/4) power (9.09% ^ (1/4)) and the answer is 54.9%.

The payoff for a 4-team parlay that pays 11 for 1 is worse than the payoff for a 3-team parlay that pays 6.5 for 1 because you need a higher winning percentage per game in order to break even with the 4-team parlay.

Advantage

You do have one advantage in parlay cards: The lines may not be sharp. Parlay cards are printed on Wednesday or Thursday, using current lines. When lines move after that, the lines on the parlay card no longer reflect current market conditions. The casinos realize this, and will sometimes eliminate certain games from the parlay card with signs like this: "Game #15 is off the parlay card." After a game line has moved several points, you will not get to take advantage of the old line on the parlay cards. However, a line does not have to move much for you to gain some edge. For lines that moved only slightly on the board, sportsbooks will usually keep them as printed on the parlay card. The key is to know how much of a difference a half point or a full point makes in the winning percentage. Differences in the lines between parlay cards and the current market are more valuable in NFL games, where a half-point difference can mean as much as a 5% difference in the winning percentage. Sometimes a half point can be useful in college football games. A half point is usually not worth much in basketball games, so it is rarely worthwhile to play basketball games on parlay cards.

Look for "half-point" and "ties-win" parlay cards. A game landing right on the number is a win on ties-win cards and can be a winner if you have the proper half point on a half-point card, but is a loser on "ties-lose" parlay cards. Ties-lose cards generally offer better odds but worse value.

There are certain numbers with high push rates in the NFL (see the table near the end of this section). The most frequent push number is a line of 3, where the probability of the favorite winning the game by exactly 3 is about 10%. If there are three or more NFL games with lines of 3 on a parlay card, then there might be positive-EV opportunity with half-point or ties-win cards. Here is an example.

Current lines on the board are:
ATL -3 DAL
PIT -3 NYJ
SD -3 OAK

Lines on the "half-point" parlay card shows:
ATL -2.5 DAL
PIT -3.5 NYJ
SD -2.5 OAK

Consider taking ATL -2.5, NYJ +3.5 and SD -2.5 in the parlay card, because you are getting an extra half point on each game compared to the current line.

You can figure out how often you expect to win given extra half points in these games. Let's take a look at one team first.

ATL is expected to win by exactly 3 points about 10% of the time. If the line is efficient, then ATL will cover the 3 points 45% of the time, as well as not cover the 3 points 45% of the time.

> 45%: ATL wins by 4 or more
> 10%: ATL wins by 3
> 45%: ATL wins by 1 or 2 or loses the game
> 100%: Total

Thus ATL -2.5 is a winner 55% of the time (45% + 10%). The same can be shown for NYJ +3.5 and SD -2.5. All three plays are 55% plays. Three 55% plays should all cover at the same time 16.64% of the time (55% x 55% x 55% = 16.64%). This 3-team parlay is a positive-EV bet because its winning percentage is greater than the break-even winning percentage of 15.38% for a 3-team parlay that pays 6.5 for 1.

In practice it is not usually this straightforward. The minimum number of games that must be played on most parlay cards is three, but you may not find three different lines with this much edge. In order to bet a 3-team parlay, you may have to include other plays that are not as strong. If you know the push percentages of every key point in the NFL, you can calculate whether a parlay is worthwhile. Let's say you find two games that are off by a half point versus a market line of -3.

> ATL -2.5 (current line -3)
> SD -2.5 (current line -3)

But the best you can find for a third game to include in your 3-team parlay is this one:

> IND -6.5 (current line -7)

For the IND game you need to know the approximate push percentage of NFL games lined at 7. If it is worth 5%, then that means IND -6.5 is a 52.5% winner (assuming IND -7 is a fair line). 52.5% is less than the 53.58% break-even winning percentage, but this game may still be useful as a filler to complete the 3-team parlay. The combination of two 55% games and one 52.5% game has value. The expected winning percentage of this combination is 15.88% (55% x 55% x 52.5% = 15.88%).

If there are two 55% games, then a third game of 50.85% makes the 3-team parlay paying 6.5 for 1 into a zero EV bet (55% x 55% x 50.85% = 15.38%). If one game is 55% and two games are 52.5%, then there is negative value in the parlay (55% x 52.5% x 52.5% = 15.16%). 15.16% is below 15.38%, thus there is slight negative EV in this 3-team parlay. However, if you happen to have an opinion on some games and want to bet them individually anyway, then the parlay card may be a good alternative to making straight plays at -110 juice.

Another issue to consider is when the accompanying money line on the point spread is not -110. Here is an example.

BAL -3 -120 CHI
CHI +3 +100 BAL

The line is shaded towards BAL -3, and the fair market line is BAL -3 -110. In that case, if you see BAL -2.5 on the parlay card, then it is greater than a 55% play. An estimate is 57.4% (52.4% reflects -110 and add 5% for the extra half point). On the other hand, if the parlay card has CHI +3.5, then it is a worse than a 55% play, at about 52.6% (47.6% + 5% = 52.6%). You will have to keep abreast of the current lines and know how to adjust the expected winning percentages based on the accompanying vig.

Profitability

Let's use the example of a 3-team "ties win" parlay that pays 6.5 for 1. There are currently three NFL games lined right at 3. In that case, the expected winning percentage of the 3-team parlay is 16.64%. If the wager is for $100, then the EV is:

= ($550 x 16.64%) + (-$100 x (100% - 16.64%))
= ($550 x 16.64%) + (-$100 x 83.36%)
= $91.52 - $83.36
= $8.16 or an ROI of 8.16%.

If the best payoff you can find is 6 for 1, then the parlay has no value.

= ($500 x 16.64%) + (-$100 x (100% - 16.64%))
= $83.20 - $83.36
= -$0.16

Betting

Casinos make adjustments, especially after suffering heavy losses. In the case of parlay cards, casinos keep an eye on games where the line has moved. When a line moves enough, the game may be taken off the parlay cards.

For smaller line changes, the sportsbooks may leave the games alone. But if you try to bet large on parlay cards, the sportsbook may refuse the wager. Unlike the limits on normal games, $500 is considered a large amount on parlay cards at most sportsbooks. Clerks often have to get approval from supervisors in order to print tickets of that value on parlay cards. The supervisor will look to see which games you picked. Smart (but nasty) supervisors will accept parlay cards filled with square bets, but refuse parlay cards filled with sharp bets. The squares get their negative-EV bets accepted while the sharps get their positive-EV bets rejected.

It is work to bet parlay cards profitably for a large amount of money. Due to the low dollar amount that most sportsbooks accept in sharp action on parlay cards, you make small wagers. In order to bet a large amount, you make bets at many sportsbooks. That involves a lot of driving and walking in the hot Las Vegas sun.

Push Percentages

Using data from NFL games from 1989 to 2006, I calculated the approximate push percentage for each point spread, as shown in table 6. I used games lined within one of the point spread; that is, I used games that were at most one point higher and one point lower than the "Line" in table 6. Then I counted the number of pushes in those games, assuming the line was the same as the point spread in all of the games for that subset. I also calculated the value of a half-point, in cents.

For example, with a point spread of the home team as a +7 underdog, I looked at all 266 games where the home team was an underdog from +6 to +8. In 6.8% of those games the home team lost by exactly 7. The standard error on that 6.8% is 1.5%, so plus and minus one standard error is 5.3% to 8.3%. The value for the half point for that line is 15 cents with a standard error of 3 cents.

The numbers are based on small sample sizes, as are most numbers generated from NFL games since each team only plays

Table 6
NFL Full-Game Push Percentages

Line	n	Push Pct	se	Half Pt	se
+7	266	6.8%	1.5%	15	3
+6	294	2.0%	0.8%	4	2
+5	260	3.1%	1.1%	6	2
+4	588	3.2%	0.7%	7	2
+3	647	9.6%	1.2%	21	3
+2	616	1.8%	0.5%	4	1
+1	281	1.4%	0.7%	3	1
pk	261	0.4%	0.4%	1	1
-1	350	2.9%	0.9%	6	2
-2	865	2.0%	0.5%	4	1
-3	1049	10.2%	0.9%	23	2
-4	988	2.3%	0.5%	5	1
-5	627	2.4%	0.6%	5	1
-6	799	2.8%	0.6%	6	1
-7	781	4.4%	0.7%	9	2
-8	628	2.4%	0.6%	5	1
-9	418	0.5%	0.3%	1	1
-10	372	4.3%	1.1%	9	2
-11	259	1.5%	0.8%	3	2
-12	163	0.6%	0.6%	1	1

Key:

All lines are from the standpoint of the home team.

Line is full-game line.

n is sample size.

Push Pct is push percentage.

Half Pt is the value (in cents) of a half point.

se is the standard error applicable to the number preceding it.

16 games a year. You may feel more comfortable smoothing out the numbers. For example, it does not make much sense that the push percentage for +1 is 1.4% while for -1 it is 2.9%. A reasonable adjustment might be to change +1 to 2.0% and -1 to 2.3%.

Local Parlay Cards

One Friday night while 2,000 miles from Nevada, I noticed a parlay card on the counter of a restaurant. Apparently the card was printed by a local bookmaker. It shocked me to see how bad the payoffs were:

> 4 Teams: 9 to 1
> 5 Teams: 15 to 1
> 6 Teams: 25 to 1

Fair odds assuming a 50% win rate per game should be:

> 4 Teams: 15 to 1
> 5 Teams: 31 to 1
> 6 Teams: 63 to 1

In order for their payouts to be fair value, one would need to have the following average win rate for each game in the parlay:

> 4 Teams: 56.2%
> 5 Teams: 57.4%
> 6 Teams: 58.1%

It was actually worse than that, as the parlay card specified ties lose, and all the games had point spreads as whole numbers. None of the lines on the card were half-point lines. Any game that landed on the number would be an automatic loser for both sides. For example, when the printed line is 3, the bookmaker is in effect dealing a line of -3.5 to the players taking the favorite and +2.5 to the players taking the underdog. As bad as the sportsbooks in Las Vegas can be to their customers, local bookmakers may be even worse, as this parlay card shows!

CHAPTER 10
NFL FIRST
HALVES

The NFL first-half bet has been popular for a while; it was one of the first derivative wagers offered that did not depend on the final outcome of the game. The interaction between line makers and bettors over the years has reduced the number of profitable opportunities, but there are still some good bets to be made.

Historical Data

Table 7 shows actual first-half results broken down by game lines for all NFL games from 1989 to 2006, including playoffs (but no Super Bowls).

The game line (GL) is in the left-most column, and is the full-game point spread from the viewpoint of the home team. It summarizes all games going off at that number plus or minus 1. For example, the line for GL = +7 includes all games for which the home team was a dog of +6 to +8 inclusive. The one exception is the PK line (PK means pick 'em); that line summarizes all games lined at +2 to -2.

Table 7
NFL First-Half Data

GL	AGL	n	+5	+4.5	+4	+3.5	+3	+2.5	+2	+1.5	+1	+0.5	pk	-0.5	-1	-1.5
+7	+6.9	263	-101	100	111	122	139					169	201	220		
+6	+6.2	294		-101	109	119	134					163	198	220		
+5	+4.9	260			106	113	124	134				157	196	221		
+4	+3.5	588				-136	-122	-106	-105	-103		107	135	160		
+3	+3.1	647					-137	-120	-118	-116	-110	-103	122	149		
+2	+2.4	616						-165	-144	-142	-140	-133	-124	-102	120	
pk	-0.2	558								-160	-153	-144	-121	102	107	112

GL	AGL	n	+0.5	pk	-0.5	-1	-1.5	-2	-2.5	-3	-3.5	-4	-4.5	-5	-5.5	-6	-6.5	-7
-2	-2.4	865	-145	-123	-101	102	105	107	109	132								
-3	-3.1	1049	-160	-137	-112			-105	-104	-102	113	127						
-4	-3.6	988	-175	-149	-118					-109	-108	104	116					
-5	-5.0	627	-197	-161	-118					-107	-106	104	114	130				
-6	-6.3	799	-221	-188	-142						-127	-113	102	115	128			
-7	-6.9	781	-232	-204	-159							-107	105	118	121			
-8	-7.7	628	-263	-233	-179								-127	-114	-101	101	103	
-9	-9.0	418	-291	-261	-201									-120	-119	-110	-101	
-10	-9.9	372	-318	-290	-226										-133	-125	-116	105

The second column, labeled AGL, is the average game line of all games in that row. For example, the +7 row summarizes all games in which the home team was +6 to +8, and the average home team in that range was +6.9. Most ranges have averages close to the midpoint of the range, but two lines stand out: game lines in the -4 row averages -3.6, and game lines in the +4 row averages +3.5. This is due to more games lined at exactly +3 (308) than +3.5 to +5 combined (280) and almost as many games lined at exactly -3 (429) as games lined from -3.5 to -5 (558).

The third column, labeled n, is the sample size, the number of games with the game line of that row.

Actual first-half game-result data are shown for each of several possible first-half lines. These numbers represent the break-even values on the games that were played. For example, if there were 500 games in a particular category, and at halftime the home team was ahead of the spread shown in the column heading in 300 of those games and was behind the spread in the other 200 games, the number in table 7 would be -150.

Pick 'em lines, flanked by +0.5 and -0.5 lines, are also shown in table 7 for every range because some sportsbooks offer money lines on first-half bets.

Here is an example of using table 7. For home teams that were -3 favorites (meaning -2 to -4 with an average of -3.1): in the first halves the home team covered -2.5 at a rate equivalent to -102; it covered a first-half line of pick 'em at a rate equivalent to -137.

The lines of table 7 are based on sample sizes ranging from 260 to 1049. When using historical numbers with small sample sizes to help value lines of games yet to be played, you should always allow a healthy margin of error. Table 7 presents three-digit numbers because sportsbooks always use three-digit numbers on their lines. However, the third digits in table 7 are meaningless, and even the second digit could be off by 1 or 2.

There are some inconsistencies apparent in the data in table 7. For example, there appear to be overly large differences between game lines of +5 and +4. Part of such differences is caused by sample sizes being small. Another part of that difference is the average game lines sometimes differ from the game line in the first column. For example, the +4 line has an average game line of +3.5 while the +5 line has an average game line of +4.9, a 1.4 difference, which is a bigger difference than average.

Just as small home underdogs have historically covered the game point spread more often than small home favorites have, small home underdogs also covered the first-half point spreads more often. For example, a -2 home favorite covered a -1 first-half line at a rate equivalent to +102; but a +2 home underdog covered a +1 first-half line at a rate equivalent to -133.

Table 8 presents one selected first-half line for each game line from table 7. These are the first-half lines most commonly used by sportsbooks for the given game line. These lines are from the point of view of the home team.

The last column of table 8, labeled se, is the standard error applicable to the terms, and depends on the sample size for that row. (Sample sizes are shown in table 7.) For example, a game line

Table 8
NFL Lines: Game vs First Half

game line	first-half line	se
7	+4 +111	12
6	+3.5 +119	12
5	+3 +124	12
4	+2.5 -106	8
3	+1 -110	8
2	PK -102	8
Pk	-0.5 +102	8
-2	-1 +102	7
-3	-2.5 -102	6
-4	-3 +104	6
-5	-3 +104	8
-6	-3.5 +102	7
-7	-4 +105	7
-8	-4.5 -101	8
-9	-6 -110	10
-10	-6.5 -116	10

of -10 is associated with a first-half line of -6.5 -116, with a standard error of 10 cents. Thus that first-half line plus or minus one standard error would be -6.5 -106 to -6.5 -126. You are welcome to smooth out the relationship between game lines and first-half lines, using the se column as a guideline for how much smoothing is appropriate.

Table 9 presents the estimated value of a half point for first-half lines according to historical game data, and is derived from table 7. The "Line" column represents the most logical whole number first-half line that sportsbooks normally use. The "Push Pct" column represents the historical percentages of first-half pushes given the first-half line. The "Half Pt" column represents the value of a half-point in terms of cents given the push percentages.

Table 9
NFL First-Half Push Percentages

Line	n	Push Pct	se	Half Pt	se
4	266	4.9%	1.3%	10	3
3	388	4.7%	1.1%	10	2
2	865	0.8%	0.3%	2	1
1	616	2.9%	0.7%	6	1
pk	568	9.5%	1.2%	21	3
-1	865	1.5%	0.4%	3	1
-2	1426	0.9%	0.2%	2	0
-3	998	5.6%	0.7%	12	2
-4	781	5.9%	0.8%	13	2
-5	628	1.0%	0.4%	2	1
-6	553	3.7%	0.8%	8	2
-7	295	8.8%	1.6%	20	4

Key:

All lines are from the standpoint of the home team.

Line is first-half line.

n is sample size applicable to that row.

Push Pct is push percentage.

Half Pt is the value (in cents) of a half point around the first-half line number.

se is the standard error applicable to the number preceding it.

For example, if a pick 'em line in the first half is -125, then the bet has a 9.5% chance of being a push and resulting in a refund. The standard error on that 9.5% is 1.2%, so think of the 9.5% as meaning somewhere in the interval of 8.3% to 10.7%. The value of a half point around pick 'em is 21 cents, with a standard error of 3 cents. Thus if a pick 'em line in the first half is -125, then the -0.5 line should be somewhere around -101 to -107, and the +0.5 line should be somewhere around -143 to -149.

The Value of Particular Numbers

Frequencies of score differences at the half differ considerably from the full-game frequencies.

Tied at the half

There are no 0.5 full-game NFL lines because ties are rare. Lines will move from pick 'em to -1 or to +1 and skip -0.5 and +0.5. But ties are not rare at the half; 9.5% of NFL games predicted to be close (and 9.1% of all NFL games) from 1989 to 2006 were tied at the half.

Sportsbooks may differ in their first-half line with some books using a pick 'em line while other books using a -0.5 or a +0.5 line. Because of the high percentage of games tied at the half, there is tremendous value in getting an extra half point (or not laying the extra half point).

3-point lead at the half

The favorite winning by 3 is by far the most common full-game result. Leading by 3 at the half is not as common. The 5.6% push percentage for the 3 is one of the highest in the first half, but it pales in comparison to the push percentage of 10.2% for the full game.

First-half lines close to 3 are common. One sportsbook may have the first-half line at home team -3 -110, while another may have it at -3.5 +100. Table 9 shows that the value of a half-point when the home team is -3 in the first half is 12 cents plus or minus 2 cents; so it likely is worthwhile to lay the extra juice and take -3 -110.

Other valuable numbers

The first-half push percentages for the 4 and 7 are both high: 5.9% for the 4; and 8.8% for the 7.

The push percentages for the 4 and 7 are both significantly higher in the first half than for the game. (Compare Table 6 with Table 9.)

Changing Times

In 2004 it was routine to find -6 -110 in the first half when the home teams were -10 favorites. Table 7 shows that based on historical data, the vig in the first half on -6 should be -125. I figured I had about 15 cents of edge and I was happy to bet -6 -110. In other relative-value plays (such as the first quarter point spread), often the positive-EV side is on the underdog. This made the -6 -110 bets in the first half especially appealing because it hedged other positive-EV relative-value bets I made on the underdog. Two bets that are both positive EV and hedging each other is pretty sweet.

But sportsbooks learn and adapt. By 2006, these opportunities were shrinking. More often than not, when home teams were -10 favorites, the first-half lines were closer to -6.5 -120.

Other Uses for Table 7

Weaker sportsbooks may move their first-half lines due to small action. If a square bets the wrong side for an amount that the sportsbook considers large (but not necessarily an amount that you would consider large), the sportsbook may move the line to a point where there is positive value for you to jump in and play.

When the game line is moved, sportsbooks may be slow to move the first-half line. Many sportsbooks are slow to move the money line when they move the point spread; the first-half lines are even farther from their minds. This strategy can be particularly valuable when a line has been taken off the board due to a potential injury. Once the injury news is known, if the new line is considerably different from the old line, then the first-half line should be adjusted also. But some sportsbooks reopen the game line and forget to adjust the first-half line until someone makes a bet. They may catch the error and refuse the bet, or they may take the bet and then change the line. A good relationship with the sportsbook manager will help in situations like this.

When you have an opinion on a game and you are looking to make a wager, compare the first-half line to the game line; there may be more value in the first-half line. For example, if the line is the Vikings -5 -110 in the game, but the first-half line is the Vikings -2.5 -110, table 7 shows that there is better value in betting the first half. It may turn out that the Vikings cover the 5 points in the game but don't cover the 2.5 points in the first half, thus turning a winner into a loser; but it is more likely for the Vikings to cover the 2.5 points in the first half and not cover the 5 points in the game, turning a loser into a winner.

Caution Using Table 7

It may be best not to rely on table 7 if you think there is some-thing specific about the game that is different from an average game with respect to the first half versus the second half. For example, say a team has lost two double-digit leads in the second half in the last few games. These collapses are going to be on their minds. If they are up big in the first half again, they may be less likely to let up in the second half. If the point spread in the game reflects this attitude, then the relationship of the game line to the first-half line may not be like that of the average game shown in table 7.

A team has a playoff spot and position locked up going into the last week of the regular season may not play to win as it normally would. Sometimes the first-string players will play only a portion of the game while the back-up players play most of it. These teams do not have winning as a primary goal, so the relationship between the first half and the game will not be like a typical NFL regular-season game. The tables in this chapter are not applicable for those games.

Conclusion

There are still some opportunities in first-half lines, but they have decreased over the years as sportsbooks and bettors get more sophisticated. But the data in this chapter can still be useful in comparing value for half-point differences in first-half lines as well as comparing relative value between game lines and first-half lines.

CHAPTER 11
OFFICE POOLS

Office pools, or football squares as they are sometimes called, are popular during NFL playoffs, especially the Super Bowl. For most people, buying a square is all luck and no skill. However, it is possible to buy, sell and trade squares with positive EV.

A 10 by 10 empty grid is passed around to the potential buyers of squares. Neither the columns nor the rows are numbered until all the squares are filled in. Buyers print their names in the empty squares, with each buyer paying the same price per square. Once all the squares are sold, a random process is used to select numbers for the columns and rows. The columns represent the last digit of one team's score, and the rows represent the last digit of the other team's score. Only the last digit, the right-most digit, of each team's score matters. For example if the final score is 34 to 10, then for the purposes of the squares, the score is 4 to 0.

When the numbers are filled in, all square owners are given a copy of the sheet so they know which numbers they have.

The payout rules should be preset before the grid is filled out. The rules can vary; some variations are:

☐ The final score of the game determines one winner and one winner only.

☐ The score at the end of each quarter determines four different winners with each winning the same amount. If the game goes into overtime, the final score takes place of the score at the end of the fourth quarter.

☐ The score at the end of each quarter determines four different winners, but the four winners pay off at different rates which are spelled out explicitly.

Good, Bad and Average Numbers

Once the columns and rows are filled in by a random process, square owners know what they are rooting for. Since football scores are predominantly field goals and touchdowns (with made extra points), the numbers that are produced by combinations of 3 and 7 are the most likely numbers to hit. In general, here are the good numbers, average numbers and bad numbers:

> Good numbers: 0, 3, 6 and 7
> Average numbers: 1 and 4
> Bad numbers: 2, 5, 8, and 9

In general, any combination that includes a bad number means the square is a dud; any combination with two good numbers is great; and any combination with one good number and one average number is okay.

Valuation of Each Square

Using a database of 4,522 NFL regular-season and playoff games from 1989 to 2006 with final scores at the end of each quarter, I was able to calculate the percentage that each square has hit. These data are not applicable for college football games, which have their own dynamic. I looked at the end of each of the first three quarters and the end of the game. If there was an overtime period, I used the final score of the game, not the score at the end of the fourth quarter, as most squares pay out this way.

Table 10 reflects the score at the end of the first quarter. The top row represents the last digit in the home team's score. The left column represents the last digit in the away team's score. The

Table 10
NFL Home & Away Scores, 1Q

a\h	0	1	2	3	4	5	6	7	8	9
0	20.7%	0.5%	0.2%	10.5%	4.0%	0.1%	1.5%	13.8%	0.1%	0.3%
1	0.2%	0.0%	0.0%	0.0%	0.0%	0.0%	0.0%	0.0%	0.0%	0.0%
2	0.1%	0.0%	0.0%	0.1%	0.0%	0.0%	0.0%	0.1%	0.0%	0.0%
3	9.0%	0.1%	0.0%	3.1%	0.8%	0.0%	0.4%	4.9%	0.0%	0.1%
4	2.6%	0.1%	0.0%	0.6%	0.2%	0.0%	0.0%	1.0%	0.0%	0.0%
5	0.1%	0.0%	0.0%	0.0%	0.0%	0.0%	0.0%	0.0%	0.0%	0.0%
6	0.9%	0.0%	0.0%	0.4%	0.0%	0.0%	0.0%	0.5%	0.0%	0.0%
7	10.1%	0.2%	0.0%	3.8%	1.5%	0.0%	0.4%	6.4%	0.0%	0.1%
8	0.0%	0.0%	0.0%	0.0%	0.0%	0.0%	0.0%	0.0%	0.0%	0.0%
9	0.2%	0.0%	0.0%	0.0%	0.0%	0.0%	0.0%	0.0%	0.0%	0.0%

numbers represent the percentage occurrences at the end of the first quarter for all NFL games during 1989-2006.

The square with the highest occurring percentage at the end of the first quarter is 0-0. This should be no surprise, as 0-0 can occur if the first quarter is scoreless or if the score is 10-0, 0-10 or 10-10.

Most of the squares that have 1, 2, 5, 8 or 9 are 0% or close to 0%.

Squares with combinations involving any of these numbers are good: 0, 3, 7.

At the end of the first quarter, 4 is an okay number, and 6 is not a good number (although it is an okay number at the end of other quarters).

The Super Bowl is played on a field selected years in advance. Unless the local team happens to qualify, the field is neutral; there is no home team. Squares are most popular for the Super Bowl, but the data are mostly from regular season games. To adjust the regular season games to fit the Super Bowl, I averaged the percentages with the same set of numbers into the same square in the rest of the tables in the chapter. For example, instead of listing the individual percentage for both 0,7 and 7,0, I averaged them and put the average in the 7,0 square. The assumption is that owners of the

0,7 and 7,0 squares have equal chances. This may not be the case for an expected blowout; more on that later in the chapter.

Tables 11-14 show frequencies of scores at the end of the first quarter, the second quarter, the third quarter and the end of the game.

Table 11
Frequency of NFL Scores, 1Q

a\h	0	1	2	3	4	5	6	7	8	9
0	20.7%									
1	0.3%	0.0%								
2	0.1%	0.0%	0.0%							
3	9.8%	0.1%	0.0%	3.1%						
4	3.3%	0.0%	0.0%	0.7%	0.2%					
5	0.1%	0.0%	0.0%	0.0%	0.0%	0.0%				
6	1.2%	0.0%	0.0%	0.4%	0.0%	0.0%	0.0%			
7	12.0%	0.1%	0.1%	4.3%	1.3%	0.0%	0.5%	6.4%		
8	0.0%	0.0%	0.0%	0.0%	0.0%	0.0%	0.0%	0.0%	0.0%	
9	0.2%	0.0%	0.0%	0.0%	0.0%	0.0%	0.0%	0.1%	0.0%	0.0%

Table 12
Frequency of NFL Scores, 2Q

a\h	0	1	2	3	4	5	6	7	8	9
0	8.0%									
1	1.1%	0.3%								
2	0.4%	0.0%	0.0%							
3	5.5%	0.8%	0.1%	3.2%						
4	3.6%	0.5%	0.1%	2.3%	1.7%					
5	0.3%	0.0%	0.0%	0.2%	0.1%	0.0%				
6	2.2%	0.3%	0.1%	1.6%	1.0%	0.0%	0.6%			
7	5.9%	1.3%	0.2%	4.3%	2.9%	0.2%	1.7%	5.8%		
8	0.5%	0.0%	0.0%	0.2%	0.2%	0.0%	0.1%	0.5%	0.0%	
9	0.7%	0.1%	0.0%	0.4%	0.3%	0.0%	0.2%	0.4%	0.0%	0.0%

Table 11 shows that 0-0 is the most likely occurrence at the end of the first quarter at 20.7%. But in tables 12-14, the percentages are much lower at 8.0%, 4.5% and 2.3% respectively.

Table 13
Frequency of NFL Scores, 3Q

a\h	0	1	2	3	4	5	6	7	8	9
0	4.5%									
1	1.4%	0.6%								
2	0.6%	0.2%	0.0%							
3	3.7%	1.0%	0.3%	3.1%						
4	2.8%	1.3%	0.4%	2.2%	2.4%					
5	0.4%	0.2%	0.0%	0.2%	0.3%	0.1%				
6	1.8%	0.4%	0.1%	1.5%	1.2%	0.1%	0.5%			
7	5.1%	1.8%	0.5%	3.5%	3.2%	0.3%	1.6%	4.1%		
8	0.7%	0.4%	0.1%	0.5%	0.4%	0.0%	0.2%	0.7%	0.1%	
9	0.6%	0.2%	0.1%	0.5%	0.5%	0.0%	0.3%	0.7%	0.2%	0.1%

Table 14
Frequency of NFL Scores, Game

a\h	0	1	2	3	4	5	6	7	8	9
0	2.3%									
1	1.5%	0.7%								
2	0.5%	0.3%	0.0%							
3	3.3%	1.1%	0.5%	1.1%						
4	2.2%	2.2%	0.6%	1.4%	1.7%					
5	0.7%	0.3%	0.3%	0.5%	0.4%	0.2%				
6	1.6%	0.8%	0.3%	1.7%	0.9%	0.2%	0.5%			
7	4.0%	1.8%	0.6%	2.4%	3.6%	0.7%	1.0%	2.2%		
8	1.0%	1.1%	0.2%	0.6%	0.8%	0.5%	0.4%	0.8%	0.3%	
9	0.8%	0.5%	0.3%	0.7%	0.7%	0.2%	0.7%	0.8%	0.2%	0.1%

Table 15
Frequency of NFL Scores, All Qtrs

a\h	1	2	3	4	5	6	7	8	9
0	8.9%								
1	1.1%	0.4%							
2	0.4%	0.1%	0.0%						
3	5.6%	0.8%	0.2%	2.6%					
4	3.0%	1.0%	0.3%	1.7%	1.5%				
5	0.4%	0.1%	0.1%	0.2%	0.2%	0.1%			
6	1.7%	0.4%	0.1%	1.3%	0.8%	0.1%	0.4%		
7	6.8%	1.3%	0.3%	3.6%	2.7%	0.3%	1.2%	4.6%	
8	0.6%	0.4%	0.1%	0.3%	0.3%	0.1%	0.2%	0.5%	0.1%
9	0.6%	0.2%	0.1%	0.4%	0.3%	0.0%	0.3%	0.5%	0.1%	0.1%

Squares containing 1 and 4 occur infrequently at the end of the first quarter and second quarter. But they do have healthy percentages at the end of the third quarter and the game.

The bad numbers, 2, 5, 8 and 9 have horribly low percentages at the end of the first and second quarters. The percentages for the bad numbers are not high for the end of the third quarter and the game either, but they do get closer to the average of 1% per square.

Some squares have payoff schedules that equally weight the end of each of the first three quarters and the end of the game. Table 15 averages tables 11-14 to get the average percentage for each square.

Some squares have unbalanced payoff schedules. Typically, the score at the end of the game has a heavier weight, followed by the score at the end of the first half and then the scores at the end of first and third quarters. By weighting tables 11-14 appropriately, you can create a table for any unbalanced payoff schedule. Table 16 is a example; it uses the following payoff schedule:

> End of game: 4 weight
> End of the first half: 2 weight
> End of the first quarter and third quarter: 1 weight

Table 16
Frequency of NFL Scores, 1x2x1x4x

a\h	1	2	3	4	5	6	7	8	9
0	6.3%								
1	1.3%	0.5%							
2	0.4%	0.2%	0.0%						
3	4.7%	0.9%	0.3%	2.1%					
4	2.8%	1.4%	0.4%	1.7%	1.6%				
5	0.5%	0.2%	0.1%	0.3%	0.3%	0.1%			
6	1.7%	0.5%	0.2%	1.5%	0.8%	0.1%	0.5%		
7	5.6%	1.5%	0.4%	3.3%	3.1%	0.4%	1.2%	3.9%	
8	0.7%	0.6%	0.1%	0.4%	0.5%	0.2%	0.2%	0.6%	0.2%
9	0.6%	0.3%	0.2%	0.5%	0.5%	0.1%	0.4%	0.6%	0.1%	0.1%

Valuation Caveats

The tables shown in this chapter have not been adjusted for the point spread or the total. Games with higher totals have a slightly greater percentage for the bad numbers (2, 5, 8 and 9) hitting at the end of the third quarter and the game. Games with large point spreads (either a large home favorite or a large away favorite) and low totals indicate the underdog is expected to score few points. In those cases, any square with 0, 3 or 7 for the underdog increases in value.

Buying, Selling and Trading

After digits for the columns and rows are determined, the tables in this chapter can be used to get the estimated probability of any particular square winning. If an unbalanced payoff schedule is used that is different from anything presented in this chapter, you can create the table you need by taking the appropriate weighted average of tables 11-14. Once you are comfortable with an estimated probability, you could try to sell your square or buy another person's square. If used intelligently, the tables in this chapter can give you an advantage in these transactions.

Interpret the tables in this chapter with a healthy margin of error. Individual games may exhibit specific characteristics that make them different from the average game. The tables in this chapter are useful as a guide, but may not be perfect for any specific game.

CHAPTER 12
SUPER BOWL
PROPS

Super Bowl proposition bets (props) have become an annual staple for football bettors. With so many potential gamblers for just one big game, sportsbooks have learned to put up a myriad of props to satisfy their customers' appetites. Many props are unbeatable because of the vig or good lines. You cannot expect to have positive EV on a wager such as "Who will win the coin toss?" when both sides are offered at -110. But every year there are some props that you can beat.

I use a 5-step process to evaluate props.

1. Understanding the prop
2. Researching statistics
3. Applying the math
4. Adjusting for the market
5. Making refinements

As an illustration, I will apply this 5-step process to the following prop: "Will the Shortest Touchdown be over or under 1.5 Yards?"

This is a popular prop found at many sportsbooks for the Super Bowl.

Understanding the Prop

Will the shortest touchdown be over or under 1.5 yards? This prop can sound confusing. The question is: Given there is at least one touchdown in the game, will there be a 1-yard or 0-yard touchdown? A 0-yard touchdown occurs when a fumble is recovered in the end zone or an interception occurs in the end zone. A 0-yard touchdown is a rare occurrence but it did happen 8 times during the 2006 NFL regular season. It also happened twice during the 2006 AFC Conference Championship game between New England and Indianapolis as an offensive lineman for each team scored a touchdown on a fumble recovery in the end zone. If you bet the over in the wager, then you are betting there will not be a 1-yard or 0-yard touchdown in the game.

If there are no touchdowns in the game, the wager should be canceled and you get your money back. If there are no touchdowns, then there is no "shortest touchdown." This same logic is used for other type of props involving the "longest" or the "shortest" of a specific event. It is possible that some sportsbooks will mistakenly grade a wager a win or a loss even if there were no touchdowns scored, so it is up to you to make sure you are not taken advantage of by the casinos.

Some sportsbooks state what happens to the wager if there are no touchdowns scored in the game. Examples are: "must be at least one touchdown in the game" and "if there are no touchdowns in the game, then the under is the winner." Another examples is: "Will there be a touchdown of less than 1.5 yards, yes or no?" The wording of this prop implies that if no touchdown is scored, then "no" is the winner. Read all props and notes carefully as they can affect the valuation.

If you bet that the shortest touchdown will be over 1.5 yards , are you rooting for a high-scoring game or a low-scoring game? Answer: The over bettor in this prop is rooting for a low-scoring game. A lower-scoring game has fewer touchdowns. With fewer touchdowns, there is a lower chance that there is at least one touchdown that is only 1 or 0 yards. The under-1.5-yards bettor is hoping for more touchdowns. With more touchdowns, there is a higher chance that at least one of those touchdowns is for 1 or 0 yards.

Researching Statistics

How likely is a 1-yard or 0-yard touchdown compared to other touchdowns? That is the main question that needs to be answered. Unfortunately for the lazy bettor, this statistic is not normally reported by the press or websites. The hardworking bettor will put in many hours of researching box scores and database compilations. He will go through the box scores of each regular-season game. He will find out how many games had 0- or 1-yard touchdowns and the percentage of all touchdowns that had 0- or 1-yard touchdowns. He will also look specifically at the two teams in the Super Bowl to see how different their numbers are from the NFL average.

I have done this research from a database of 1,528 regular-season games from 2001 through 2006. 807 of those games had a 0- or 1-yard touchdown scored. There were no touchdowns in 14 games. And in the remaining 707 games, there were touchdowns scored, but none shorter than 1.5 yards.

For the rest of this chapter I will assume that if no touchdowns are scored in the game, the bet is canceled. 807 games with at least one 0- or 1-yard touchdown and 707 games without means 53.3% games went under 1.5 and 46.7% went over 1.5.

Another way to approach the statistics is to figure out the percentage of touchdowns that were 0- or 1-yard touchdowns. In the same 1,528 regular season games from 2001 to 2006, there were 7,209 total touchdowns scored, or an average of 4.72 per game. Of those 7,209 touchdowns, 1,078 were 0- or 1-yard touchdowns. That comes out to 15.0% of all touchdowns for 0 or 1 yard. This approach can be useful as we shall see in the next section.

Applying Math

If all games in the NFL were expected to have the same number of touchdowns, then using 53.3% for the under and 46.7% for the over would be a decent estimate. But reality is not that simple. Some games are expected to be higher scoring than others. If the overall estimate of 53.3% for the under were applied for all games, then that estimate would be too low for high-scoring games and too high for low-scoring games.

To adjust depending on the expected score of the game, use the statistic that 15% of all touchdowns are 0 or 1 yards. Consider the individual teams and their particular characteristics. It is possible the teams in the game have a much higher or a much lower expected percentage of 0- or 1-yard touchdowns than the league average; this tendency may be due to how they play the game rather than randomness. If that is the case, then using the league average to describe those teams may be a mistake. This is discussed further in the section titled "Making refinements."

First, estimate the number of touchdowns that will be scored in the game. This estimate can come from the total in the game. Usually during the Super Bowl, sportsbooks will have a line on the over/under for the number of touchdowns scored and the number of field goals made. This information can be useful for relative-value comparison purposes.

Next, calculate the expected number of 0- or 1-yard touchdowns that will be scored in the game. If the expected number of touchdowns is 5.0, and you believe 15% of all touchdowns are 0- or 1-yard touchdowns, then the expected number of 0- or 1-yard touchdowns is 0.75 (5 x 15%).

This prop looks like it fits the Poisson distribution. The following is the explanation of the Poisson distribution in Stanford Wong's *Sharp Sports Betting*, pp. 151-152 (2006 printing).

The two properties necessary for the Poisson distribution to apply to the number of events are: 1. The event must be something that is counted one at a time, and 2. The probability of occurrence of the event is small, while the number of attempts to achieve the event is large.

See Stanford Wong's *Sharp Sports Betting* for more information on applying the Poisson distribution to sports betting as well as SharpSportsBetting.com to download an Excel spreadsheet. The number of touchdowns under 1.5 yards fit the above description. It happens one at a time and the probability of occurrence of the event is small, but it can theoretically happen on any play of the game.

Using the Poisson distribution, first figure out the probability of zero touchdowns scored in the game. Since no touchdowns means

Table 17
Shortest NFL TD will be O/U 1.5 yards?

TDs	1 yd	0 TD	1 no	1 yes	A no	A yes	Over	Under
3	0.45	5.0%	63.8%	36.2%	61.9%	38.1%	-162	162
3.5	0.53	3.0%	59.2%	40.8%	57.9%	42.1%	-138	138
4	0.60	1.8%	54.9%	45.1%	54.1%	45.9%	-118	118
4.5	0.68	1.1%	50.9%	49.1%	50.4%	49.6%	-101	101
5	0.75	0.7%	47.2%	52.8%	46.8%	53.2%	114	-114
5.5	0.83	0.4%	43.8%	56.2%	43.6%	56.4%	129	-129
6	0.90	0.2%	40.7%	59.3%	40.6%	59.4%	146	-146

Key:

TDs: expected number of touchdowns

1 yd: TDs x 15%; expected number of 0- or 1-yard touchdowns.

0 TD: the probability there is no touchdown

1 no: the probability that no 0- or 1-yard touchdown will occur.

1 yes: the probability that a 0- or 1-yard touchdown will occur.

A no: taking out the games with zero touchdowns. Adjusting the "no" probability for pushes when there are 0 TDs.

A yes: taking out the games with zero touchdowns. Adjusting the "yes" probability for pushes when there are 0 TDs.

Over: Shortest TD will be over 1.5 yards, converted to a money line format

Under: Shortest TD will be under 1.5 yards, converted to a money line format

a push for the wager, it is important to take that probability out of the equation.

Table 17 shows the results given the number of expected touchdowns. As more touchdowns are expected to be scored, there is an increase in the probability of a 0- or 1-yard touchdown. Thus the under becomes more and more of a favorite down the table.

Different props require different mathematical methods. The steps in this section are a good model for similar props, such as:

Will the shortest field goal be over or under 24.5 yards?
Will the longest kickoff return be over or under 33.5 yards?
Will the longest pass completion be over or under 38.5 yards?

Even with a good estimate, you still need to be cautious and give your self a comfortable margin of error. It is always possible you made a calculation error, misapplied theory, or made a bad assumption. In fact, this is what happened to me when I first wrote about this prop for the *Two Plus Two Internet Magazine*. I made an error and misapplied the math. I was shown my error by Jesse Gregory, who responded in a thread on SharpSportsBetting.com. The error was subtle but important. In my original analysis, my incorrect estimate was not that far off from the corrected estimate, thus I did not bet too much on my mistake. But even if my incorrect estimate had been wrong by a large margin, I would not have bet a lot because I always build in a comfortable margin for error. I would also consult a friend to double-check my work to see if I am missing something. Although it is possible to win betting against the sportsbooks, do not underestimate the lines the sportsbooks put up. Make the bets, but accept that it is possible you are the one making the mistake, and not the sportsbook.

Adjusting for the Market

Adjusting for market conditions is important. Using the averages during the regular season for the two teams in the Super Bowl may lead to mistakes. If the total on the Super Bowl indicates a different expectation of the number of touchdowns scored in the game than the averages for the two teams in the regular season, then the total on the Super Bowl is a better number to use because it is a market number.

Even if you think the total on the game is too high or too low, and want to make a bet on the total, it is still important to use the market number for the total in your expected touchdown estimates because you do not want to derivatively bet the total at a worse number than the total itself. For example, the total on the game is 50 and you think that is too high and want to bet the under. It would be a mistake to bet "the shortest touchdown will be over 1.5 yards" at a level appropriate for a total of 45. (Remember, betting the over on this prop means you are rooting for a low-scoring game.) Then you would be derivatively betting under 45 via the prop bet, when instead you should be happier with betting under 50 in the total.

Making Refinements

There are many refinements that you may wish to make based on the specific teams, point spread and total in the game. These refinements can make a difference, but the research is much more involved. Some possible questions to answer are: Is a passing team less likely to score a 1-yard touchdown? Are specific teams more likely to run when in the red zone, and if so, are they more likely to score 1-yard touchdowns than other teams? What do you do if the two teams in the game have an unusually low (or high) number of 1-yard touchdowns in this past year? Is that an aberration or is it something that is consistent with their specific styles of play? This is the Super Bowl, but you are looking at regular season statistics. Are there differences between the regular season and the playoffs (especially the Super Bowl) that may make the regular-season statistics moot? These are tough questions to answer. It shows that even with some research and application of the math, there is still some subjectivity involved in figuring out fair value.

Blocked Punts Prop

Here is an example of a prop that I bet before the 2007 Super Bowl between the Colts and the Bears. I bet against a long shot to occur:

Under 0.5 Blocked Punts -800

I think the true price should have been -1880. Blocked punts happen in about 5% of all NFL games, but sportsbooks offered the prop as if the frequency were 11%. I calculated my EV as:

EV of under 0.5 blocked punts at -800
= ($100 x 95%) – ($800 x 5%)
= $55

The ROI on this prop was 6.9% ($55/$800).

Table 18 contains statistics from NFL.com that support the estimate that 5% of NFL games have a punt blocked. In the four NFL regular seasons prior to that Super Bowl, a total of 1,024 games had 53 blocked punts.

Table 18
NFL Blocked Punts

year	number
2006	12
2005	9
2004	11
2003	21

It is also important to look at the teams in the game. If they had blocked more punts or had more of their punts blocked, then this could be a bad wager. This was not the case with the Bears and the Colts. Neither the Bears nor the Colts had any punts blocked in 2006. The Colts blocked one punt, and the Bears blocked none. That is a total of one blocked punt in 32 games between the two teams, which is lower than the 5% rate for the rest of the NFL.

Weather can be a factor. Rain was forecast for the Super Bowl between the Colts and the Bears. Games played in the rain or on a wet surface may mean slicker footballs that are tougher to handle. This may lead to more dropped snaps by punters, which may lead to a higher chance of a blocked punt in the game. But a slick field also makes it tougher for punt blockers to get to the punter quickly. I was comfortable with my wager in spite of the weather forecast.

Copycat Gets Punished

While shopping for prop bets in Las Vegas for the 2006 Super Bowl between Seattle and Pittsburgh, I visited a sportsbook that I knew copied prop lines from other sportsbooks. The copycat would wait a few days after the originating sportsbooks had their props listed, to allow time for sharp bettors to bet into any weak lines and move them to their proper levels. In essence, the copycat was allowing the originating sportsbooks to shoulder the expense of fine-tuning the lines.

I was not optimistic about finding any positive EV bets as I knew the book's modus operandi. But then I ran across one prop that seemed way off.

Seattle punts before scoring:
    Yes +150
    No -180

I jumped on the Yes right away because I knew it was positive EV. I made sure I did not misread the prop; yet I did not want to waste any time in case another sharp bettor also noticed it. I wondered how the book could make that mistake when it was simply copying some other sportsbook's prop. Later that night I realized what had happened when I found this prop at another sportsbook:

Seattle punts twice before scoring:
    Yes +150
    No -180

I thought this line was close to fair value. The difference was the word "twice." The copycat forgot to copy that word, and it changed the probabilities of the prop.

CHAPTER 13
MARCH
MADNESS
POOLS

March Madness bracket pools are popular annual events. Many people who do not normally bet on sports get involved. It takes luck to win, and the more people in the pool, the more luck required.

There are methods to gain advantages over other participants. These methods do not require the ability to handicap games.

The two goals to focus on when making March Madness bracket picks are:

☐ Picking teams more likely to win

☐ Separating yourself from the pack by picking teams that are picked by fewer participants

The teams are seeded #1 to #16, making it easy to identify the favorites. (For the rest of this chapter, the *lower seed* will mean the team with the lower seed number, the team the selection committee thinks is the better team; the *higher seed* will mean its opponent, the team with the higher seed number. So in a game between seeds #5 and #12, the #5 seed is the lower seed and the #12 seed is the higher seed.)

You can get information by looking at the relative seeds. The lower seed is usually the better team and thus the favorite to win the game. The bigger the difference between seed numbers, the bigger the difference between teams.

Picking teams that are more likely to win is easy to understand. #1 and #2 seeds have good chances of reaching the Final Four; #15 and #16 seeds are unlikely to make the Sweet Sixteen.

Separating yourself from the pack is possible if a team picked by you but by few others wins a game. When that happens, you get a leg up on many other participants. You do not care about having a great record so much as you care about having the *only* great record. Most pools pay only the winner or the top few places. In a pool with 100 participants, placing 10th, 50th or 100th all pay off the same amount: nothing.

The problem with separating yourself from the pack by making a pick that differs from the rest of the participants is that it generally requires picking teams more likely to lose. Fortunately there are teams you can pick that are favorites in spite of most other participants picking their opponents. This happens because the seeding is done by a committee, and the committee sometimes makes mistakes. Betting lines are more accurate than seedings.

March Madness attracts many people who do not normally bet on sports. Such participants may be unaware of the betting lines on the games, and simply assume the lower seed is the favorite, and thus be inclined to pick that team. Generally they are correct, but not always. In some games the higher seed is the favorite in the betting line. These are the games where it is possible to gain separation from your opponents while picking teams more likely to win. This is market information that is readily available but not taken into account by most participants. Betting lines can be found in many daily newspapers and on the Internet.

The First Round

When you look at first-round betting lines, some games will jump out. A #10 seed might be a favorite over a #7 seed. In that situation, the #10 seed has a higher chance of winning the game. Picking the #10 seed helps achieve both goals.

The matchups where the higher seed might possibly be the betting favorite are:

> #9 vs. #8
> #10 vs. #7
> #11 vs. #6

Higher seeds that are small underdogs (2 points or less) in the betting line can also be useful in separating yourself from the pack while picking teams with reasonable chances of winning. This is more useful when the difference in the seeds is greater. Taking a small underdog is more useful if the dog is a #11 seed than if it's a #9 seed. Fewer other participants are going to join you in picking a #11 seed than a #9 seed because a #11 seed seems like a bigger underdog to them. Here is an example.

> East Region:
> #6 seed -10
> #11 seed +10
> West Region:
> #6 seed -2
> #11 seed +2

In the East Region, taking the #11 seed hurts your chances of being in the prize money since it is a 10-point underdog, and 10-point underdogs seldom win the game. In the West Region, the #11 seed is a 2-point dog; meaning it has a reasonable chance of winning the game. Other participants in the pool may consider both #6 seeds are equally likely to win their respective games. Picking a small underdog (with the help of the betting line) is a way to separate yourself from the pack. In picking the #11 seed in the West Region, you pick a team only slightly more likely to lose than to win, but can gain in separation.

There are websites that allow pool participants to make their bracket picks online. These websites are easy to use, popular among participants, and often free. Some of these websites indicate the percentage of pool participants that picked certain teams. This information is useful in identifying teams that can help separate yourself from the pack.

The Second Round

You will not know the betting lines for the second-round games before the first-round games are played. But you can make educated guesses on the betting lines in the second round. A good tool to use is power ratings. These can be found in some newspapers and on the Internet. Not all power ratings are good, so determine how accurately a power rating reflects the betting line. See if the power rating's projected lines for the first round are close to the actual lines. If they are close, then they are likely to be close for the second round. Sometimes power ratings will show that a higher seed will be a favorite or a small underdog. This will occur most often in the matchups of the #4 vs. #5 seeds, and the #3 vs. #6 seeds. Using good power ratings, you can make similar judgments of chances of winning the games versus separation as you did in the first round.

The Third Round and Beyond

The futures market is useful in looking at the third round and beyond. Look for teams that may be high seeded but are given a good shot at winning their region. Usually the favorites in each region will appear right in line with their respective seeds. The #1 seed will be the biggest favorite, followed by the #2 seed and then the #3 and #4 seeds. But sometimes a higher seed will have the same or better chance of winning the region than a lower seed. It may be due to where they are playing; for example, a #3 team could be playing close to home whereas the #2 seed could be far from home, so the #3 team enjoys a home court advantage. There could be other causes too, such as a mistake in seed placements by the tournament committee.

When a sportsbook offers two-sided lines, allowing you to bet against as well as on certain teams to win their region, the odds information is useful. But most sportsbooks offer one-sided lines, allowing you to bet on a team but not allowing bets that the team will not win its region or the whole tournament. When only one-sided odds are offered, the odds are not as informative and could be misleading. The high vigorish in one-sided futures lines can result in odds that do not truly reflect a team's chance of winning. Two teams, each of which is offered at +200 to win the region, do not necessarily have equal chances if only one-sided lines are offered.

2006 March Madness

Most of this chapter was previously published in *Two Plus Two Internet Magazine* a couple of weeks before the 2006 March Madness tournament. When the teams and matchups for the tournament were set, I wrote a few thoughts about specific matchups as a follow-up to that article in my blog. Here is the post I wrote in my blog, edited only for spelling and grammar. The sections in [] are results known after the tournament.

In the first round, I suggested to look at higher seeds that were favorites or small underdogs in the betting lines. The idea is that most competitors in pools do not understand the value of betting lines and use seed numbers and name recognition for their picks. The early lines show nine games with lines of 2.5 or lower. Although all the lower (better) seeded teams are the favorites, some of them are surprisingly small favorites.

Here are games where taking the underdog probably gives you value in separating from the pack while giving up little chance of winning the game.

Texas A&M vs. Syracuse: #12 vs. #5

Syracuse is a #5 seed, and Texas A&M is a #12 seed, but Syracuse is only a 1.5 point favorite! That is tiny for such a big difference in seedings. Syracuse also has the better college basketball name, having won NCAA championships in the past. Syracuse just made a miraculous run and won the Big East Tournament, which was featured widely on ESPN and other sports channels. Picking Texas A&M probably gets a lot of bang for the buck, separating yourself from the pack while giving up little in individual-game expectancy.

[#12 Texas A&M beats #5 Syracuse 66-58]

Wisconsin-Milwaukee vs. Oklahoma: #11 vs. #6

Wisconsin-Milwaukee is a #11 seed and is only a 2-point dog to Oklahoma, the #6 seed. Oklahoma is from a big conference, is well known in college sports, and is regularly among the best teams in basketball and football. Pickers likely will take Oklahoma due to its seed and its name recognition.

[#11 Wisconsin-Milwaukee beats #6 Oklahoma 82-74]

San Diego State vs. Indiana: #11 vs. #6

Indiana is a big name in college basketball, whereas San Diego State is not. Yet San Diego State is only a 2.5 point dog. Although picking San Diego State is giving up a little bit more in line value, it is probably gaining more than its worth in separation value.

[#6 Indiana beats #11 San Diego State 87-83]

Wisconsin vs. Arizona: #9 vs. #8

UAB vs. Kentucky: #9 vs. #8

Arizona is a 1.5 point favorite while Kentucky is a 2 point favorite. Picking a #9 seed may not achieve much separation since the small difference in the seedings allows laymen more reason to pick the underdog. In these two cases, both #8 seeds are big-time college basketball powerhouses. So in these two cases, picking the underdog is likely to get more separation value than other typical #8 vs. #9 matchups.

[#8 Arizona beats #9 Wisconsin 94-75]

[#8 Kentucky beats #9 UAB 69-64]

Here are three games where the line is low, but I have more reservations about picking the underdog.

Wichita -2.5 vs. Seton Hall: #7 vs. #10

Marquette -2 Alabama: #7 vs. #10

California -1.5 NC State #7 vs. #10

In these three matchups between the #7 and #10 seeds, all underdogs are well known as college basketball teams. A layman is more likely to pick the underdog in these matchups than in other matchups. Thus picking the underdog has less value in separating from the pack (because too many others are picking the same underdogs as you), while it still suffers from the same amount of individual-game expectancy as the previous matchups I listed.

[#7 Wichita State beats #10 Seton Hall 86-66]

[#10 Alabama beats #7 Marquette 90-85]

[#10 NC State beats #7 California 58-52]

Notes on two regionals

Oakland Region

The #3, #4 and #5 seeds all seem to be valued the same. Gonzaga, Kansas and Pittsburgh are all getting the same respect in futures lines. So taking Pittsburgh (the #5 seed) to proceed further in the tournament than Gonzaga (the #3 seed) probably has no-cost value in separating yourself from the pack.

[#2 UCLA wins the Oakland Region]

[#5 Pittsburgh was knocked out in the second round]

[#3 Gonzaga was knocked out in the third round]

D.C. Region

From the initial lines, it looks like Tennessee and Illinois are valued about the same. Tennessee is a #2 seed and Illinois is a #4 seed. The tough issue with Illinois is that it is likely to meet the #1 seed Connecticut. I would use this information by making sure not to pick Tennessee to go too far in the tourney.

[#1 Connecticut won the D.C. Region]

[#2 Tennessee lost in the second round, after winning its first-round game by only 2 points against a #15 seed]

[#4 Illinois lost in the second round]

Conclusion

Winning a March Madness bracket pool takes luck. The more participants in the pool, the more luck required. Looking at the betting lines and futures lines can help in gaining small advantages. It is difficult to balance the two goals of picking the team more likely to win each game and trying to separate yourself from the pack. Keep in mind that with more participants in the pool, the more value there is in separating yourself from the pack and having an extreme performance. There is as much reward for finishing 10th as finishing 200th. The goal of picking teams more likely to win individual games is more important in smaller pools than in bigger pools. If you are in an office pool with people who are not avid sports bettors, then these strategies have value. If you are in a pool with people who bet sports regularly, then these strategies have less value since this group is more likely to know what the point spreads are for each game.

CHAPTER 14
NBA PLAYOFFS

A Sports Riddle

Two teams play in a best-of-seven series in which each team has exactly 50% chance of winning each game. There is no home field advantage and there is no memory of previous games (results in previous games do not affect later games). Which is more likely to occur: the series ends in six games or the series ends in seven games?

Try to answer this question without doing any math. Try to use logic only. Do not read further until you have given it some thought.

Most people's gut-feel answer is that the series is more likely to end in seven games than six games. Since the teams are equally matched, it feels like the series will be closely played. There is no closer series than a 4-3 series.

The correct answer is that the series is equally likely to end in six or seven games. Brute force can be used to crank out all the possibilities and come up with that answer. But a logical answer with no math involved is more elegant and interesting.

Two questions will help to get the logical answer: How can a series end in seven games? How can a series get to 3-3?

☐ How can a series end in seven games? Answer: the series must be tied 3-3 in order for the seventh game to be played.

☐ How can a series get to 3-3? Answer: the series can get to a 3-3 tie only when one team is ahead 3-2.

Putting these two together, you see that if a team that is ahead 3-2 wins the sixth game, then it wins the series. If the team that is ahead 3-2 loses the sixth game, then the series will go to the seventh game. If each team has a 50% chance of winning each game, the team ahead 3-2 in the series has a 50% chance of winning game 6 and ending the series in 6 games. Conversely, the team ahead 3-2 in the series has a 50% chance of losing game 6, which means a seventh game will be played.

In real life this may not be directly applicable, because teams and players do have memories and there is usually an advantage to playing at home. The NBA home-court advantage is large, so it often matters which team is at home and what the series results are going into Game 6. NBA teams have the tendency to play better and win more often after a bad game in the playoffs. The informally named zigzag theory explains this effect.

Zigzag Theory

The simplest form of the zigzag theory in the NBA playoffs is: The team that lost a game is likely to cover the spread in the next game. For example, if the Lakers lost to the Suns in game 1 of a playoff series, the zigzag theory suggests betting on the Lakers to cover in game 2.

From a database of NBA playoff games from 2000 to 2006 (other results in this chapter uses the same set of data), the zigzag theory's record was 231-211 for a winning percentage of 52.3%, basically break-even for -110 lines.

A refinement to the zigzag theory is to add in the qualification that the losing team did not cover the point spread in the previous game. With that refinement, the zigzag theory's record was 190-163 for a winning percentage of 53.8%. Data miners can get better winning percentages with more refinements, but testing them runs into the problem of small sample sizes.

I do not recommend you bet the zigzag theory based on this discussion alone. Line makers learn from history and sportsbooks adjust to action. Because the zigzag theory is well known, line makers probably have a good handle on its historical performance. Lines in the NBA playoffs may already have the zigzag factor embedded in them. Thus blindly betting the zigzag theory may be negative EV in future games.

The next two sections present historical against-the-spread (ATS) records and line changes from game to game, which are more important. Bigger line changes than in the past suggest that the zigzag theory is embedded in the line.

Must-Win Games

Must-win games are games where a loss results in the end of the series or falling behind so much that it is nearly impossible to come back. The lines in these games often lean towards the team that needs the win.

Game 3, home team down 0-2

In 54 games, the home team has a straight-up record of 34-20 and an ATS record of 34-19-1. The average line in these game 3s was the home team laying 0.65 points.

In game 4 of those same series after the home team won game 3, the average line shifted to the home team getting 0.21 points. That game-to-game line shift of 0.86 points indicates that the betting market is aware of the must-win situation in game 3 for home teams down 0-2.

Game 4, home team down 0-3

This is a must-win situation. If the home team loses, it is out of the playoffs. But instead of playing harder, as generally happens in must-win situations, the 0-3 home team seems to play with less intensity. Perhaps the players think that being down 0-3 is too large of a hole to dig out of. No NBA playoff team has ever come back from a 0-3 deficit to win the series.

The database shows 15 games where the home team was down 0-3. In those 15 games, the average line was home team +3.47, up from an average line of +0.67 in the game 3. (The average over all game 3s with a 0-2 home team was home team -0.65; +0.67 applies to only the subset of those game in which the home team lost game 3.) That is a whopping game-to-game line shift of

2.8 points! The market expects a team down 0-3 to give less than full effort. Even with the extra points, the home team has had a tough time covering; its game-4 ATS record was 5-9-1. That sample size is too small for us to draw firm conclusions.

Game 6, home team down 2-3

When the home team is down 2 games to 3 going into game 6, the average line has the home team laying 1.8 points. In game 4 when the same team is at home (without counting the NBA Finals when game 4 and 6 have different home teams), the average spread is home team by 1.2 points. Thus the home team is favored by 0.6 extra points in game 6 when down 2-3 in the series. The must-win situation is probably the reason for this difference.

Game 7

Game 7 is the deciding game of the series; it is a must-win game for both teams. Both games 5 and 7 are played in the same venue, so it is interesting to compare the difference in the point spreads in those two games. Only 19 game 7s were played in the NBA from 2000 to 2006 (without counting the NBA Finals when game 5 and 7 have different home teams), but even with this small sample size, the line movement is interesting.

Averaging the lines in all game 7s, the home team was a 4.5 point favorite. In the average game 5 in every series that had a game 7, the home team was a 5.3 point favorite. The home team was a smaller favorite in game 7 by 0.8 points. In those 19 instances of game 7, the home team had an ATS record of 11-7-1. Perhaps the market erred in making the home team less of a favorite in game 7, but the sample size is too small to say for sure. The average line shift from game 5 to game 7 may be useful in calculating exact series lines.

Exact Series Lines

For playoff series in the NBA, NHL, and MLB, sportsbooks often offer money lines on which team wins the series as well as exact series lines, which are lines on whether a certain team will win the series in a specific number of games. For example: "Yankees to win the ALCS in six games +150." If the Yankees win the ALCS, but not in six games, then this bet is a loser.

A sportsbook may update the series money line and the exact series lines after every game. The series money line and the exact series lines are connected. The money lines for the individual games are connected to both the series money line and the exact series lines. Sometimes a sportsbook puts up lines that conflict with each other. You can take advantage of these situations by understanding how these three bets are connected. The current game line is likely the most efficient because the most money is being bet on it. Try to predict lines for the games yet to be played. Then calculate the series money line as well as the exact series lines for all possibilities. The difficult part is predicting the lines in the games yet to be played. Here is an example.

It is the 2006 NBA playoffs and the Mavericks are playing the Suns in the Western Conference Finals. The series is tied 2-2 with games 5 and 7 (if necessary) in Dallas and game 6 in Phoenix. The mid-market money line on game 5 is the Mavericks -300, indicating the market thinks the Mavericks have a 75% chance of winning game 5. In order to estimate the series line and the exact series lines, you must project the expected money lines for games 6 and 7. Here are my projections and the reasoning behind them.

Game 6

In games 3 and 4, with the Suns at home, the line was the Suns pick 'em and +1, respectively. Game 6 is a different situation because it will be an elimination game for one team or the other. Since the Mavericks are heavy favorites to win game 5, the Suns are more likely to be the team facing elimination in game 6. Thus the line for game 6 is expected to be tilted more towards the Suns than games 3 and 4, and they are likely to be favored.

If the Mavericks win game 5, it would not be surprising to see the Suns as a 1 point favorite in game 6. The Suns will get more respect from the line makers and bettors due to the emotional factor of having their backs to the wall in an elimination game. Also, the zigzag theory is well known in the NBA playoffs; most bettors and bookmakers expect the team behind in the series to play with more energy and focus.

On the other hand, if the Suns win game 5, then it would not be surprising to see the Mavericks as a 1 point favorite in game 6. The Mavericks would have the emotional energy to play harder.

A 1 point favorite equates to -107 in the money line or 51.7%. If the Mavericks win game 5, they will be pegged with a 48.3% chance to win game 6. If the Mavericks lose game 5, then they will be pegged with a 51.7% chance to win game 6.

Game 7

In order for there to be game 7, the Suns and Mavericks must win one game apiece in games 5 and 6. For game 7, the zigzag theory will no longer affect the line because it is an elimination game for both teams. Thus game 7 should differ from game 5 in that both teams should be equally motivated. In game 5, the Mavericks are a 7 point favorite, or -300 in the money line. Let's make them favored by less in game 7; make them a 6.5 point favorite and -270 in the money line (73%).

Calculations

Now you have all the numbers needed to make the calculations. These numbers assume there are no injuries to the key players or other factors that could cause a big change in market perception.

Game 5: Mavericks 75%, Suns 25%
Game 6 if the Suns win game 5: Mavericks 51.7%, Suns 48.3%
Game 6 if the Mavericks win game 5: Mavericks 48.3%, Suns 51.7%
Game 7: Mavericks 73%, Suns 27%

Here are the ways that the Mavericks can win the series and their corresponding percentages:

Scenario 1
    Game 5: Win 75%
    Game 6: Win 48.3%
    75% x 48.3% = 36.2%

Scenario 2
    Game 5: Win 75%
    Game 6: Lose 51.7%
    Game 7: Win 73%
    75% x 51.7% x 73% = 28.3%

Scenario 3
> Game 5: Lose 25%
> Game 6: Win 51.7%
> Game 7: Win 73%
> 25% x 51.7% x 73% = 9.4%

Add up the percentages in all three scenarios, and the probability that the Mavericks win the series is 73.9%.

> 36.2% + 28.3% + 9.4%
> = 73.9% or -283

The series money line at a major sportsbook before Game 5 was Mavericks -310, Suns +270. The numbers calculated above are right in line with the market. In general, series lines are fairly efficient; it is tough to find an edge big enough to bet on.

With only three games left, it is easier to evaluate the exact series lines than before the series started. With the numbers above, the calculations for the exact series lines are as follows.

Mavericks win in 6 games:
> = 75% x 48.3%
> = 36.2% or +176

Mavericks win in 7 games:
> = (75% x 51.7% x 73%) + (25% x 51.7% x 73%)
> = 28.3% + 9.4%
> = 37.7% or +165

Suns win in 6 games:
> = 25% x 48.3%
> = 12.1% or +726

Suns win in 7 games:
> = (25% x 51.7% x 27%) + (75% x 51.7% x 27%)
> = 3.5% + 10.5%
> = 14.0% or +614

Check to see if the lines are consistent with each other in case you made an arithmetic error. Add the probability of the Mavericks winning in 6 and 7 games, and see if it is the same answer as the Mavericks to win the series. In this case it is.

Mavericks in 6 + Mavericks in 7 = Mavericks to win the series
    36.2% + 37.7% = 73.9%

Suns in 6 + Suns in 7 = Suns to win the series
    12.1% + 14.0% = 26.1%

73.9% + 26.1% = 100%

Generally only sharper sportsbooks offer updated lines on exact series lines. However, you can sometimes find value. After game 4, I was able to find one sportsbook offering the Mavericks in 6 at +200. I bet it since I thought I had 24 cents of edge.

I won the bet when the Mavericks won the series in game 6. After the Mavericks won game 5, the game-6 line opened with the Suns -1 , as I expected. The line drifted to Suns -1.5 by game time, so my edge might have been smaller than 24 cents.

Exact Series Line Spreadsheet

I wrote an Excel spreadsheet to calculate the exact series line and the series money line in the NBA playoffs with user inputs of the point spread in each game. The spreadsheet can be found at SharpSportsBetting.com in the Prop Tools link.

CHAPTER 15
BASEBALL:
FIRST HALVES

Betting on the first half has been popular in football and basketball for several years. A few creative sportsbooks are now offering a similar line for baseball. A sportsbook offering a new bet can make mistakes due to inexperience and incomplete understanding of the nuances of the new bet. The book may even put up a wrong line if simply copying another sportsbook's lines. This chapter examines the value of first-half lines relative to game lines for baseball.

Some sportsbooks define the first half of a baseball game as the first five innings; others define it as the first 4.5 innings. Some sportsbooks offer these wagers with a money line; others offer them with a half-run line. Here are the types of first half baseball lines that will be covered in this chapter:

☐ Money line on the first five full innings
☐ Money line on the first 4.5 innings
☐ Favorite laying a half run in the first five full innings

For good baseball handicappers, the first-half line may be easier to handicap as there are fewer variables, such as relief pitchers, pinch hitters and managerial maneuvers. The information in this chapter may not be as useful to good baseball handicappers since they already have the ability to handicap the first five innings without the need for historical database information.

Without handicapping, you can still get a good idea of the value of a first-half line by comparing it to the game line, given the assumption that the game line is efficient. This can be done by looking at the historical relationship between the game line and the results in the first half. But before looking at that relationship, let's take a look at some issues that separate game probabilities from first half probabilities.

First Half Versus Full Game

The probabilities of a team winning the game and the team winning after five innings are related, but they also differ in predictable ways. Here are some issues to consider for individual games.

Endurance of starting pitchers

Starting pitchers do not pitch as well in the late innings as they do in the early innings. Some pitchers decline faster than others. Although a fantastic pitcher, Pedro Martinez no longer pitches many innings relative to his peers, and needs more help from the bullpen. This is a factor when betting on or against him in a game, but it is not a concern in the first-half wager since it is likely he will pitch all five innings. Looking at the average innings pitched by the starting pitchers can help in seeing how the first-half line and the game line differ.

Here is a hypothetical example. In late September, the Mets have already clinched the NL East and they are playing the Marlins. Pedro Martinez is in line for his last start of the regular season, and is slated to start the first game of the playoffs, a week away. Mets manager Willie Randolph has been known to be careful with Martinez's arm, and is likely to do so in this game too. He publicly stated that Martinez is going to throw five innings and then be pulled out of the game no matter the score. The sixth and seventh innings will be pitched by middle-relievers. Game lines are fairly efficient, and the market adjusts for this information. Normally this match-up might be Mets -200, but with the information that Martinez is going to pitch only five innings, the game line is Mets -160. Since Martinez is going to pitch the first five innings, the relationship between the first half and the full game will be skewed in this game. Instead of the first half being related to a game with a line of -160, it is probably more related to a game with a line of -200.

Bullpen strengths of teams

Although relief pitchers are not often used in the first five innings, it is still useful to understand the relative strength of the bullpens. Large differences in relative bullpen strengths can skew the relationship between the game line and the first-half line. An example is the 1996 Yankees, who had Mariano Rivera pitching in the setup role and John Wetteland as the closer. In the playoffs, when the Yankees had a lead, Rivera would pitch the seventh and eighth innings and Wetteland would pitch the ninth inning. If the Yankees had a lead after six innings, they were difficult to beat because of these two fantastic relievers. But these fantastic relief pitchers have no relevance to the first-half line since they are not used in the first five innings.

It is also useful to understand if certain relievers are available for the particular game in the regular season. If Trevor Hoffman has pitched in three straight games in the regular season, the San Diego Padres may opt to sit him out of the fourth game regardless of the situation. There is likely a big drop-off from Hoffman to his replacement that night. Other relievers may have a problem pitching two days in a row if they are coming off of injuries. Billy Wagner was an example of that in the early part of 2006. Sportsbooks may incorporate these factors into the game odds, but they are immaterial for the first-half line.

Bench strength for pinch-hitting

Some teams have stronger bench players. A team with solid bats on the bench may be better equipped in the late innings when pinch hitters are used more often. This is especially important in the National League, where starting pitchers are often replaced by pinch hitters in the sixth inning and beyond. In the first half of the game, the bench is rarely a factor. The money line on the game may incorporate the relative strengths of the bench, but bench strength is not of consequence in the first-half line.

Sometimes a regular starter is not in the starting lineup but is available to pinch-hit. Critical pinch-hitting appearances normally come after the fifth inning. Barry Bonds is often rested for day games after night games but he can still be called to pinch-hit. The Giants may still get a plate appearance from him in the game (and possibly more if he takes the field afterwards) but his pinch-hitting appearance will be after the fifth inning. In this case, the first half line should favor the Giants' opponent slightly relative to the game line.

Five Innings

The most popular first-half line in baseball is the line on the first five full innings. My approach to evaluating this line is to compare it to the game money line and then incorporate individual game factors afterwards to see if anything needs to be adjusted for the specific game situation.

Using historical data to compare the results of the first five innings to the results of the game yields a guide to valuing first-half lines. Table 19 summarizes historical data for Major League Baseball games from 2000 to 2006 from the home team's perspective. The table shows the money line range (Home ML), the implied win percentage as calculated from the average money lines (Implied Win %) and the actual winning percentage in the full game and the first five innings. Games tied after five innings are omitted.

Table 19
Win Rates MLB Full Game and 5 Innings

Home ML	Implied Win%	Full Game	5 Innings%	Sample Size
-300 to -201	-232 or 69.9%	-231 or 69.8%	-200 or 66.7%	1080
-200 to -176	-188 or 65.3%	-184 or 64.8%	-175 or 63.7%	1086
-175 to -151	-162 or 61.8%	-167 or 62.5%	-156 or 60.9%	1975
-150 to -126	-138 or 57.9%	-131 or 56.8%	-129 or 56.3%	3121
-125 to 100	-112 or 52.8%	-114 or 53.2%	-115 or 53.4%	3817
101 to 125	112 or 47.1%	110 or 47.7%	110 or 47.6%	2610
126 to 150	137 or 42.2%	134 or 42.7%	129 or 43.7%	1572
151 to 175	162 or 38.2%	149 or 40.1%	132 or 43.1%	684

The results for the first five innings closely resemble the game results. When the money line is -150 to +150, it appears that the line for the first five full innings should be identical to the game money line. This is unfortunate for bettors because it means the bookmakers are not in error by copying the game line for the first-half line. But bookmakers can make mistakes, and mistakes can be made on games where the money line is more extreme than -150 for either team.

The deviations are in the extremes when the game money line is beyond -150 for either team. Big underdogs do better in the first five innings than they do in the game. If the sportsbook does not adjust correctly, it may be better to bet a big underdog in the first five inning line than in the game line.

4.5 Innings

Some sportsbooks define the first half as the first 4.5 innings. They do not count the home team's at bats in the bottom of the fifth inning. This wager is unbalanced in that the away team gets five chances to hit while the home team gets four. Naturally the road team gets an advantage in this line.

Table 20 compares the results for 4.5 innings with five innings (sorted by game line). The data cover the same time frame as table 19.

As expected, the away team does better in a 4.5-inning line than in a five-inning line. On average, the away team wins 7.9% more often in the first 4.5-inning line than against the five-inning line.

Table 20
Win Rates MLB 5 and 4.5 Innings

Home ML	5 Innings	4.5 Innings	Difference
-300 to -201	-200 or 66.7%	-146 or 59.4%	-54 or 7.3%
-200 to -176	-175 or 63.7%	-127 or 56.0%	-48 or 7.7%
-175 to -151	-156 or 60.9%	-109 or 52.1%	-47 or 8.8%
-150 to -126	-129 or 56.3%	108 or 48.0%	-37 or 8.3%
-125 to 100	-115 or 53.4%	122 or 45.0%	-37 or 8.4%
101 to 125	110 or 47.6%	153 or 39.5%	-43 or 8.1%
126 to 150	129 or 43.7%	172 or 36.7%	-44 or 7.0%
151 to 175	132 or 43.1%	179 or 35.8%	-47 or 7.3%

Table 21
MLB Half-Run Lines for 5 Innings

Home ML	5 Innings	Home -0.5	Diff	Home +0.5	Diff
-300 to -201	-200 or 66.7%	-132 or 56.9%	-68 or -9.8%		
-200 to -176	-175 or 63.7%	-121 or 54.8%	-54 or -8.9%		
-175 to -151	-156 or 60.9%	-112 or 52.9%	-43 or -8.0%		
-150 to -126	-129 or 56.3%	105 or 48.8%	-34 or -7.5%		
-125 to 100	-115 or 53.4%	120 or 45.4%	-35 or -8.0%		
101 to 125	110 or 47.6%			-123 or 55.1%	33 or 7.5%
126 to 150	129 or 43.7%			-107 or 51.7%	36 or 8.0%
151 to 175	132 or 43.1%			-103 or 50.7%	35 or 7.6%

Half Runs in Five Innings

Some sportsbooks use a half-run line as their first-half line. A half-run line has winners and losers, no ties. Typically the favorite lays the half run.

Table 21 compares money lines, five-inning lines, and the five-inning lines with the favorite laying a half run. For brevity the table shows only the relevant numbers.

The difference between the money line and the half-run line seems to be fairly constant at about 8%. There is a larger difference when the game money line is -300 to -201, but just slightly more than 1000 games fell into that range, so the differences may be due to the small sample size.

Conclusion

First-half betting in baseball is relatively new. As more sportsbooks offer these lines, opportunities may exist, even if you do not handicap. But opportunities do not last long in sports betting. Savvy bettors jump at positive-EV bets and bookmakers learn quickly.

First-half betting is an example of new proposition bets in baseball. Your job is to find them, evaluate them and then beat them.

CHAPTER 16 BASEBALL: TOTALS

Totals are bet on major-league baseball games. You can bet whether the combined scores of both teams will be over or under a number, henceforth referred to as the *betting total* so as not to confuse it with the actual total of the game. If the actual total is the same as the betting total, then the bet is a push. Sometimes different sportsbooks will have different betting totals on the same game. The vigs on the over and under are typically adjusted to price the difference so there is no clear arbitrage or obvious middle opportunity. Here is an example of two different totals at two sportsbooks.

STL vs LAD

Sportsbook A	*Sportsbook B*
Over 7 -130	Over 7.5 -105
Under 7 +110	Under 7.5 -115

At Sportsbook A you can bet over 7, but must lay 130 to win 100. At Sportsbook B you cannot bet over 7; that option is not available. If you want to bet the over, the betting total at Sportsbook B is 7.5. The vig on the over is friendlier to compensate for the half-run difference; you risk 105 to win 100.

Once you have decided on a particular wager, how do you figure out which line is best? If you are looking to bet the over, then betting over 7 seems better because you will push if the actual total is 7. Betting over 7.5 means you will lose if the actual total is 7. But you risk less to win the same amount. Given the difference in the vig, which one is the better bet? This chapter answers this question.

MLB Total Push Rates

Using a database of games and totals from 1998 to 2006, I was able to calculate the push percentages for games that had betting totals within a half-run of the actual total. For example, I looked at the percentage of games that landed exactly on 7 when the betting total was 6.5, 7 and 7.5. Table 22 shows the results, which are from a database of more than 21,000 games with betting totals of 6.5 to 11.5. The numbers do not differentiate between leagues, teams, game lines or any other situation.

Table 22
MLB Totals: Betting to Actual

bet\actual	7	8	9	10	11
7	13.5%				
7.5	11.8%	6.5%			
8		8.2%			
8.5		6.9%	10.0%		
9			10.8%		
9.5			10.0%	6.2%	
10				6.7%	
10.5				6.6%	9.2%
11					8.8%
11.5					7.4%
Average	12.4%	7.2%	10.3%	6.5%	8.9%
se	0.8%	0.3%	0.3%	0.3%	0.5%

The left column is the betting total. The top row is the actual total. For example 13.5% of games that had a betting total of 7 landed exactly on 7. The 6.5 row is not shown because the sample size is only 57 games.

The differences between columns are significant. As for the differences between rows, there is significance in that an integer betting total is more likely to have the actual total fall right on the number than is a betting total a half game away.

The number in the Average row is the average of all relevant games for the actual total from all games with the appropriate betting line. The se row shows the standard errors of the numbers in the Average row.

More Odds than Evens

Baseball totals are more likely to be odd score than even. This is intuitively logical since a baseball game cannot end in a tie; tie games always have even totals. When the score is tied after 9 innings, the teams keep playing until there is a winner. A game cannot end in a 4-4 tie, but can end with one team winning 5-4. This means games are more likely to end with odd totals (7 and 9) than even totals (8 and 10). For example the actual total is 7 during 12.4% of its relevant games (betting totals of 6.5, 7 and 7.5), while the actual total is 8 during 7.2% of its relevant games (betting totals of 7.5, 8 and 8.5).

Higher Totals Have Fewer Pushes

A higher betting total is associated with a wider distribution of actual totals. Thus the chance of any specific actual total happening decreases. As the betting total increases, the chance that the actual total lands on the betting total decreases.

Since odd totals happen more often than even totals, it is fair to compare odd totals to each other and even totals to each other. Comparing odd totals, 12.4% of relevant games land on 7 (betting totals of 6.5 to 7.5), while 10.3% of relevant games land on 9. Comparing even totals, 7.2% of relevant games land on 8, while 6.5% of relevant games land on 10. The higher the total, the less likely the game is to land right on the number.

Value Depends on the Total

The next step is to transform these data into money-line differentials for half-run differences in betting totals. Look at totals of 6.5 to 7.5 to see the values of the half-runs 6.5 to 7 and 7 to 7.5.

Assume the following:

☐   The fair value total is exactly 7

☐   Based on the data, you believe 13.5% of these games will have an actual total of 7

Using the above assumptions, 43.25% of the games land below 7, another 43.25% of the games land above 7, and the remaining 13.5% are exactly 7. This balance makes over 7 and under 7 have equal value, as stated in the assumptions.

Runs Scored	Probability
1-6	43.25%
7	13.50%
8+	43.25%
Total	100%

Over 6.5 has a 56.75% chance of winning as you sum the chances of the total being 7 and 8+ (13.50% + 43.25%). In the money line, 56.75% equals -131. As a rule of thumb, the half-run around the 7 is worth about 31 cents in the money line.

Using the rule of thumb of 31 cents, if the fair value on a betting total is over 7 -120, then over 6.5 is worth -151. Over 7.5 is worth +111 (See Chapter 2 for the rules of adding/subtracting cents when the numbers cross +100/-100.)

Using the rule of thumb, these three lines have equivalent value:

Over 6.5 -151
Over 7 -120
Over 7.5 +111

The rule of thumb is less accurate the farther the line is from even money (+100). Rules of thumb are useful when comparing betting totals on the fly. If you have time and a computer or calculator handy, working out the math will be more exact. But if you are in a Las Vegas sportsbook or do not have much time before the game starts, then use the rule of thumb.

Table 23
MLB Half-Run Values

Total	Half-run	+/- .5 runs
7	31 cents	28 cents
8	18 cents	16 cents
9	24 cents	23 cents
10	14 cents	14 cents
11	19 cents	19 cents

The push rate of 13.5%, which is the percentage of games with betting totals of 7 that landed exactly on 7, was used to create the half-run value of 31 cents. But other information exists in the form of betting totals of 6.5 and 7.5. The percentage of all games with totals from 6.5 to 7.5 that landed exactly on 7 was 12.4%. If 12.4% is used instead of 13.5%, the value of a half-run off the 7 is 28 cents.

Using the same process to create rules of thumb for other betting totals gives the values shown in table 23. The "Half-run" column shows the value of a half run using whole-number betting totals. The "+/- .5 runs" column shows the value of a half run using betting totals plus or minus half a run.

Notice that the half-run value is higher when the betting total is odd than when it is even. This reflects more games ending with odd totals than even.

An example with totals of 7 / 7.5

You now have enough information to determine which sportsbook offers better value depending on whether you want to bet the over or the under.

STL vs LAD

Sportsbook A	Sportsbook B
Over 7 -130	Over 7.5 -105
Under 7 +110	Under 7.5 -115

Assume you want to bet the over. Although you are laying less vig by taking over 7.5 at -105 compared to over 7 at -130, it is not worth the risk for the 25 cents you save on the vig. Table 23 shows that the half-run increase from 7 to 7.5 is worth 31 cents. If you are going to bet the over, the over 7 -130 is a better value than over 7.5 -105. The equivalent of over 7 -130 is over 7.5 +101. (Using money line cents math, -130 plus 31 cents = +101.)

On the other hand, if you like the under, you should bet under 7.5 -115. The 7 is worth 31 cents, so under 7 +110 is equivalent to under 7.5 -121. (+110 minus 31 cents = -121.)

An example with totals of 10 / 10.5

Suppose the betting totals are 10 and 10.5 at different sportsbooks, but with the same vigs as the previous example.

CLE vs KC

Sportsbook A	Sportsbook B
Over 10 -130	Over 10.5 -105
Under 10 +110	Under 10.5 -115

Table 23 shows that the half-run value off the 10 is worth 14 cents. In this case, taking over 10.5 -105 has better value than over 10 -130. Over 10.5 -105 is equivalent to over 10 -119. (-105 plus -14 = -119.) If you want to bet the over, take the 10.5 in this example.

If you like the under, take under 10 +110. Under 10 +110 is equivalent to under 10.5 -104. (+110 plus -14 = -104.) In order to take under 10.5 at Sportsbook B, you must lay -115. Under 10 +110 has better value.

Notice the difference in these two examples. Although the vig differences are the same in the two games, the over bet with more value in the first example is over 7 -130, but in the second example, it is over 10.5 -105. The difference in the half-run value between the 7 and the 10 causes a different optimal bet. Consider both the vig difference and the value of the half-run to determine which line provides better value.

Conclusion

There is a higher chance of a game landing on an odd total. There is a lower chance of a game landing on a specific total when the betting total increases. We calculated the value of a half-run for two sample betting totals. You can use this information to choose among different betting totals.

CHAPTER 17
RACING'S
TRIPLE CROWN

A popular proposition bet in horse racing is: Will a horse win the Triple Crown this year? Bettors can bet on "Yes" or "No." For the "Yes" to win this bet, the same horse must win the three races in the Triple Crown: the Kentucky Derby, the Preakness and the Belmont Stakes. Books that offer this prop will typically offer it throughout the three races as long as the "Yes" is still live. Here is an example of the wager in a typical year where there are no huge favorites.

Before the Kentucky Derby

Will a horse win the Triple Crown?
    Yes +700
    No -1000

The sharp bettor's initial thought is that the "No" is a positive-EV bet. It is common knowledge that no horse has won the Triple Crown since 1978. It is also typical in prop bets with long odds that the side laying heavy money has an edge. An example is the "no overtime" prop in the Super Bowl, which is a good overlay at -1000 or better, and is usually widely available. Most people look at long-shot wagers with a lottery mentality. It is human nature to be will-ing to risk a small amount to try for a big payoff, but not the oppo-site, even if that opposite has positive EV. Few people are willing to risk $1,000 to try to win $100. The bookmakers know that they are likely to take more bets on the long shot. So they are happy to shade the line before they get any action. An event where the true odds on the "No" are -2000 could possibly be -1000 at sports-books. For these reasons, at first glance the "No" on the Triple Crown bet looks attractive to the sharp bettor.

Wait! Do not run to your sportsbook and plunk down any money on this "No" bet just yet. Kentucky Derby winners always be-come fan favorites and always see their odds decrease (implying a greater chance of winning) in the other two legs of the Triple Crown. Each win gains a horse more respect in the marketplace. "No" bettors can often bet into more favorable lines by waiting until after the Kentucky Derby. Even if the "No" has positive EV be-fore the Kentucky Derby, you are better off waiting until after the Kentucky Derby to make the "No" bet. I will explain why this is so throughout the rest of this chapter.

Bet the "No" after the Derby

The "No" on the Triple Crown before the Kentucky Derby is not a good bet because there will be better opportunities to make the same bet after the Kentucky Derby. After the Kentucky Derby, people focus on the winner. The race is analyzed by handicappers, stories are told via the media, and the Derby winner looks better and better. Any horse that wins a race usually looks good in doing so. If the winning horse was not a favorite in the Kentucky Derby, people find reasons why the horse did not do better in previous races, thus trying to justify the Derby win as the race that showed the true talents of the horse. The horse is being held in the highest regard of its career.

The attention then focuses on whether the horse can win the Preakness. There is only one more race after the Preakness for the Triple Crown, so the talk naturally also includes whether the horse can win the Triple Crown. ESPN, newspapers, and anyone covering horse racing will ponder this question, talking about it over and over. Viewers and readers gobble it up. This is a good time to consider betting the "No Triple Crown Winner" prop.

If a Favorite Wins the Derby

When one of the favorites in the Kentucky Derby wins the race, that horse will be an even greater favorite in the Preakness. If the horse also wins the Preakness, then he will be a monumental favorite in the Belmont Stakes.

Table 24 shows the Kentucky Derby winners from 1986 to 2005 that won the Kentucky Derby with odds lower than 10-1. These are races where one of the favorites wins. The odds listed are pari-mutuel odds and have a built-in vigorish for the track, so the true odds are a touch higher. Since we are looking at how the odds change on the same horse in different races, I will leave the track odds as is for this section.

Notes: The "W%" columns are the odds transformed into winning percentages. Blank odds in the Belmont Stakes means the horse did not win the Preakness.

Table 24 shows that every time one of the favorites won the Kentucky Derby, it became an even greater favorite in the

Table 24
Kentucky Derby Winners Below 10-1

Year	Horse	KY Derby Odds	W%	Preakness Odds	W%	Belmont Stakes Odds	W%
2004	Smarty Jones	4.1	19.6%	0.7	58.8%	0.35	74.1%
2000	Fusaichi Pegasis	2.3	30.3%	0.3	76.9%		
1998	Real Quiet	8.4	10.6%	2.5	28.6%	0.8	55.6%
1997	Silver Charm	4.0	20.0%	3.1	24.4%	1.05	48.8%
1994	Go For Gin	9.1	9.9%	2.8	26.3%		
1991	Strike the Gold	4.8	17.2%	1.8	35.7%		
1989	Sunday Silence	3.1	24.4%	2.1	32.3%	0.9	52.6%
1988	Winning Colors	3.4	22.7%	1.9	34.5%		
1987	Alysheba	8.4	10.6%	2.0	33.3%	0.8	55.6%
Average			18.4%		39.0%		57.3%

Preakness. If it then won the Preakness, it became a greater favorite yet in the Belmont Stakes. For example, in 1987 Alysheba went from 8.4 to 1 in the Kentucky Derby to 2 to 1 in the Preakness. And in the Belmont Stakes, Alysheba was favored against the field, at 0.8 to 1.

If a Long Shot Wins the Derby

What happens when a middle-of-the-pack horse or a long shot wins the Kentucky Derby? That horse became one of the favorites in the Preakness. If it won the Preakness, it became the favorite in the Belmont Stakes. Horses gain so much respect from winning the Kentucky Derby that they are quickly advanced to the top of the class by bettors. The horses also benefit from a diminished field in the Preakness (more on that later). A middle-of-the-pack horse that wins the Kentucky Derby becomes the favorite in subsequent races. A long shot that wins the Kentucky Derby may not be the favorite in the Preakness, but will be among the favorites.

Table 25 shows the Kentucky Derby winners since 1986 that won the Kentucky Derby with odds higher than 10-1. The table

Table 25
Kentucky Derby Winners Above 10-1

		KY Derby		Preakness		Belmont Stakes	
Year	Horse	Odds	W%	Odds	W%	Odds	W%
2005	Giacomo	50.3	2.0%	6	14.3%		
2003	Funny Cide	12.8	7.3%	1.9	34.5%	1.0	50.0%
2002	War Emblem	20.5	4.7%	2.8	26.3%	1.25	44.4%
2001	Monarchos	10.5	8.7%	2.3	30.3%		
1999	Charismatic	31.3	3.1%	8.4	10.6%	1.6	38.8%
1995	Thunder Gulch	24.5	3.9%	3.8	20.8%		
1993	Sea Hero	12.9	7.2%	4.3	18.9%		
1992	Lil E. Tee	16.8	5.6%	4.2	19.2%		
1990	Unbridled	10.8	8.5%	1.7	37.0%		
1986	Ferdinand	17.7	5.4%	3.1	24.4%		
Average			5.6%		23.6%		44.3%

shows that even middle-of-the-pack and long-shot winners of the Kentucky Derby are among the favorites in the Preakness and Belmont Stakes (if they get that far). For example, in 1986 Ferdinand went from 17.7 to 1 in the Kentucky Derby to 3.1 to 1 in the Preakness.

Fewer Horses in Later Races

For Kentucky Derby winners that went off at odds less than 10-1, their average expected track winning percentage (ETW%) went from 18.4% in the Kentucky Derby to 39.0% to the Preakness. This is a healthy gain of respect, more than 100% increase in their ETW%.

The middle-of-the-pack and long-shot Kentucky Derby winners gained even more respect, relatively. They went from an average ETW% of 5.6% in the Kentucky Derby all the way up to 23.6%. That is more than a 300% increase in their ETW%. Is this newfound respect deserved? It is difficult to say with a sample size of only 20 years. Some argue it is deserved because the horses do not run many races before the Kentucky Derby. Thus any win (especially in a big field like the Derby) means something special. Additionally, even long shots that won the Kentucky Derby turned out to be quality horses for the rest of their careers. I will leave this argument for the experts in horse racing.

One additional factor that increases the chances of the Kentucky Derby winners in the Preakness and Belmont is the diminishing fields in the last two legs of the Triple Crown. Table 26 shows the average number of entrants in each race for the twenty years 1987 to 2006.

Table 26
Number of Entrants in Major Races

Race	Avg. # of Entrants
Kentucky Derby	17.0
Preakness	10.4
Belmont Stakes	9.9

On average, the Preakness has 39% fewer entrants than the Kentucky Derby. The dropout horses include both long shots and favorites. Horses that were among the favorites and also ran a good race in the Kentucky Derby (but did not win) sometimes skip the Preakness, but come back in the Belmont Stakes. For example, in 2003 Empire Maker was the favorite in the Kentucky Derby at 2.5 to 1 and finished second to Funny Cide (12.8 to 1). Empire Maker did not race in the Preakness, but did come back and win the Belmont to spoil Funny Cide's bid for the Triple Crown. Interestingly, Funny Cide was the favorite in the Belmont at 1 to 1, while Empire Maker was 2 to 1. The two wins by Funny Cide had propelled it past Empire Maker in the eyes of the bettors.

The diminished field will help the chances of any entrant winning the Preakness relative to the large field in the Kentucky Derby. The Kentucky Derby winner will usually race in the Preakness because the winner naturally had a good race in the Kentucky Derby. Also, the glory and extra prize money in winning the Triple Crown is tough to pass up. In the past 20 years only one Kentucky Derby winner did not race in the Preakness (1996 Grindstone skipped the Preakness due to a career-ending injury).

Lower Odds in the Belmont

One of the favorites winning the Kentucky Derby confirms that everyone was right about the talents of the winning horse. As shown above, the odds for the horse to win the Preakness will be low relative to the horse's odds in the Kentucky Derby. If that horse also wins the Preakness, then it will reach legendary status quickly. The odds for that horse in the Belmont Stakes will be astonishingly low and unattractive for positive-EV seekers. Table 27 lists the odds in the Belmont Stakes for the six horses since 1997 that had a chance to win the Triple Crown. Even with these low odds, none of these horses won the Triple Crown.

The average of these six horses had a 52.4% chance of winning the Triple Crown according to the track odds. None of them won. If these were true odds, the probability that none of them would win would be about 1%. It is tough to draw any conclusions on whether the lowered odds are deserved in the Belmont, as the sample size is too small. For the purpose of this prop bet, it is important to note the big drop in the odds as the horse continues to

Table 27
Belmont Stakes Odds for TC Candidates

Year	TC Candidate	Odds
2004	Smarty Jones	0.35
2003	Funny Cide	1.00
2002	War Emblem	1.25
1999	Charismatic	1.60
1998	Real Quiet	0.80
1997	Silver Charm	1.05

win. That may or may not continue in future years, but assuming it will continue is the smart way to bet.

Before the Belmont Stakes, some sportsbooks put up two-way lines on the possibility of a Triple Crown winner. This may now be a good time to bet against the possible Triple Crown winner. Many forces have come together to make the odds seem too low on the favorite. There is probably more EV in betting on the "No" at this juncture than before the Kentucky Derby.

Belmont Souvenirs

The odds for the possible Triple Crown winner are low before the Belmont Stakes due to the horse's great showings in the first two races. Adding to this is an unusual and interesting twist that occurs in the Belmont Stakes that is unique in sports. There are many horse racing fans, and many of them love making a small wager on the possible Triple Crown winner for the purpose of keeping the ticket as a collectible. These memorabilia seekers have no interest in cashing their tickets if the horse wins. They just want a keepsake to commemorate the moment, and for horse racing fans there is no better memorabilia than a winning ticket of the last leg of the Triple Crown! Although most of these memorabilia seek-ers bet the minimum $2, there are many of them, so this type of bet adds up and may affect the final odds. How much of an influence do the collectors have as a whole? It is tough to say and I do not have any figures, only anecdotal evidence. Some experts do not think collectors have a big impact. When a horse finally does win the Triple Crown, we will have a better idea as we will surely see some of these souvenir tickets for sale on eBay.

Putting the Odds Together

With all this information, we can now estimate the fair market odds for a Triple Crown winner. Even if you disagree with the market odds, it is important to consider what the market odds will be since those are the odds you can bet into. This is important for futures wagers, and important for the Triple Crown bet.

Historically, the average ETW% for the Kentucky Derby winner in the Preakness is 30.9%. That includes every horse from 1986 through 2005 except the 1996 winner Grindstone who did not race in the Preakness. Of the eight horses that had won the first two legs of the Triple Crown, the average ETW% on those horses is 52.4% in the Belmont Stakes.

Do not fall into the trap of thinking that because the Triple Crown winner has to win three races, the calculations must have three different probabilities involved. One horse will win the Kentucky Derby. That means after the Kentucky Derby, there is always a horse that can possibly win the Triple Crown. We just do not know which horse it will be until after the Kentucky Derby. Sportsbooks have fallen into this trap in the past and posted juicy lines for savvy bettors.

The track takes a large portion off the top. I will use the track take of 18% in the Preakness and 14% in the Belmont, and adjust the ETW% into an adjusted expected winning percentage. For the Belmont Stakes, I will adjust by an additional 5% due to the possible impact the memorabilia collectors have on the posted odds.

Preakness: 30.9% / 1.18 = 26.2%
Belmont Stakes: 52.4% / 1.14 / 1.05 = 43.8%
Triple Crown Winner: 26.2% x 43.8% = 11.48% or +771

If you believe the impact of the memorabilia collectors on the odds in the Belmont Stakes is tiny, then you would get:

Belmont Stakes: 52.4% / 1.14 = 46.0%
Triple Crown Winner: 26.2% x 46.0% = 12.05% or +730

The example of a typical line I showed at the beginning of this chapter now looks fair and not worth a wager. Of course, every year has a different set of horses. What I have shown here is that the "No" wager before the Kentucky Derby is not the automatic positive-EV bet that it may seem to be at first glance. In my experience the "No" has more value after the Kentucky Derby, as this is when gamblers start to think about betting on the "Yes." After the Kentucky Derby, the gamblers know the name of the horse they will be rooting for if they bet on the "Yes." As the sportsbooks get action on the "Yes," they move the line on the "Yes" and the "No." If they move the line enough, then the "No" may become attractive.

An Example From 2002

Before the Kentucky Derby, I saw this line:

Will there be a Triple Crown Winner?
Yes +700
No -1050

I thought the "No" at -1050 looked like a good bet and made a wager on it. (This was before I did the analysis shown in this chapter.) War Emblem went on to win the Kentucky Derby as a 20.5 to 1 shot in an 18-horse race. Based on the odds, eight of the horses had a better chance of winning the race. Before the Kentucky Derby, War Emblem was definitely thought to be a middle-of-the-pack horse, thus the 20.5 to 1 odds. After the Kentucky Derby, I was thrilled about the "No" bet that I made. I thought there was a good chance that War Emblem would not be the favorite in the Preakness and I felt good about my wager.

To my surprise, War Emblem went off at 2.8 to 1 in the Preakness. He was now the favorite! I noted that six of the horses in the Kentucky Derby that went off at lower odds than War Emblem did not even race in the Preakness. Before the Kentucky Derby, these six horses were considered better racers. The fact that they did not even race was a good sign for War Emblem and a bad sign for me. Luck was on War Emblem's side.

If War Emblem were to win the Preakness, I knew it would mean more bad news in the Belmont Stakes. I calculated the Triple Crown probabilities and found out I had not gained any value on my wager even when a middle-of-the-pack horse won the Kentucky Derby. It was a disaster for my "No" bet.

Odds in the Preakness: 2.8 to 1 = 26.3%
Adjusted for the track take: 26.3% / 1.18 = 22.3%

It turned out War Emblem's odds during the Belmont Stakes were 1.25 to 1, so I will use those numbers for these calculations.

Odds in the Belmont Stakes: 1.25 to 1 = 44.4%
Adjusted for the track take: 44.4% / 1.14 = 38.9%
War Emblem to win the Triple Crown: 22.3% x 38.9% = 8.67% or +1053

Recapping what happened: I made a bet that no horse would win the Triple Crown. A middle-of-the-pack horse won the Kentucky Derby, which should be good news; I was happy! But it turns out that based on the fair market value of the horses in the Preakness and the Belmont Stakes, I did not gain any value at all. Rather, the implied odds in the Triple Crown bet remained the same as the price I bet. At this point, gamblers started to bet on the "Yes." Once they had a horse they could identify with, the money flowed in on the "Yes" side. They felt War Emblem was a horse that was capable of winning the Triple Crown. In the days before the Preakness, I had the chance to bet the "No" at better odds than I did before the Kentucky Derby. I had the chance to bet the "No" at -950 and at -750! I realized that the market reactions after the Kentucky Derby made the "No" before the Kentucky Derby a bad idea. What would have happened if one of the favorites had won the Kentucky Derby? The market would have determined an even higher chance for a Triple Crown winner. It seemed the only way my "No" bet would still look good after the Kentucky Derby is if a horse with higher odds than War Emblem's 20.5 to 1 had won.

An Example From 2006

The main part of this chapter was published as an article in the May 2006 edition of the *Two Plus Two Internet Magazine*. On 8 May 2006 after the 2006 Kentucky Derby, I posted about the triple crown in my blog: http://WeighingTheOdds.blogspot.com.

BLOG Entry on 8 May 2006

The Triple Crown bet is going exactly as one would guess based on history and what happened in the Kentucky Derby. Barbaro won the Kentucky Derby as one of the favorites, and by a large margin. Now the odds on Barbaro to win the Preakness are around even money, and at some places that have two-way lines, bettors can bet against Barbaro to win the Preakness at even money! If Barbaro does win the Preakness, the odds on Barbaro to win the Belmont Stakes will surely be even lower. The current odds on the Yes for "Will there be a Triple Crown Winner" is +250. This is too cheap given that he is even money in the Preakness. I was focusing on whether there was value on the No, but instead the value given the lines in the Preakness is on the Yes.

We can see what the betting lines in the Preakness and the Triple Crown prop are implying in terms of the odds in the Belmont.

Triple Crown winner: Yes +250 = 28.57%
Barbaro to win the Preakness: No +100 = 50%
Barbaro to win the Belmont (implied): 28.57% / 50% = 57.14%

If Barbaro wins the Preakness, will the ETW% on Barbaro to win the Belmont be 57.14%? In my opinion, no, that is too low! Table 24 shows the Derby winners of 10-1 or lower odds and their odds in later races. On average they increased their ETW% by more than the 7.1% increase that the market is implying for Barbaro.

So my suggestion, if you can find these lines, is to make the following two wagers:

Bet x amount on Triple Crown Yes +250
Bet to win x amount on Barbaro to NOT win the Preakness at +100

If Barbaro does NOT win the Preakness, then you lose x on the Triple-Crown bet, but win x on the Preakness and break even.

If Barbaro does win the Preakness, then you are now basically risking a total of 2x to win 1.5x. This is equivalent to betting Barbaro at a rate of 57.1% in the Belmont, but the bet counts only if Barbaro wins the Preakness. In my opinion, the only way that will not be a good bet given Barbaro wins the Preakness is if Barbaro somehow gets injured. That is a possible risk, but a low one. If Barbaro does win the Preakness, 57.1% will look cheap for Barbaro to win the Belmont.

That blog entry was an example of handicapping future lines, as opposed to handicapping the horses. I did not have an opinion on Barbaro's chances to win the Preakness, but I did have an opinion on Barbaro's chances to win the Belmont given he won the Preakness, and that was the wager I suggested. Barbaro did not win the Preakness. Barbaro was injured early in the race and eventually had to be put down due to the injury. The combination of the two bets that I suggested resulted in a push.

Conclusion

Don't make a Triple Crown bet before the Kentucky Derby. Although it is possible the "No" can be a positive-EV wager, there probably are better opportunities to make the same bet after the Kentucky Derby. Once the Kentucky Derby is run, find out the early odds in the Preakness and think ahead and estimate the odds in the Belmont Stakes assuming the Derby winner also wins the Preakness. With these two pieces of information, you can estimate the odds of the Kentucky Derby winner winning the Triple Crown and evaluate if there are any positive-EV bets.

CHAPTER 18 FUTURES

Time Value of Money

You should consider two things before plunking down money on futures bets: the time value of money and opportunity costs.

Futures bets often take a long time to settle. If you make a Super Bowl bet in August, you cannot collect any winnings until February. Instead of putting the money into the futures bet, you could have put it in a bank and earned interest. If the interest rate is 4%, then over the course of half a year, the bank account will earn 2%. A ROI of 1% on a Super Bowl bet you make in August is a bad bet because you have a higher ROI by simply putting the money in the bank for the six months it takes for the bet to be decided. Money in the bank has a higher ROI and is risk-free!

The other problem with futures bets is that they tie up capital. Unless you are making the bets on credit or using a betting exchange, you cannot get out of your bet and sell back your position without laying out even more capital. New opportunities may arise between the time you make the futures bet and the time it is settled, and you want to have enough capital to take advantage. Opportunity costs are tough to measure because it is difficult to predict if you will need the capital. But it is a possibility, and thus there is a cost associated with long-term bets.

A silver lining to these two negative issues is that other sharp bettors also take them into consideration. Their capital is valuable as they like to put most of it in action every week, spread out among many different bets. (See chapter 24 for a statement to this effect by a Las Vegas professional bettor.) Some sharp bettors may pass on positive-EV futures bets or they may not even analyze them at all. Lines on long-term futures may stay juicy for a longer period of time as the sharp bettors concentrate on short-term wagers. When futures come closer to expiration, sharp bettors will start to analyze and bet them.

I travel to Las Vegas frequently, but I do not live there. This means I do not enjoy the same opportunities that Las Vegas bettors enjoy. Living in Las Vegas, the local sharp bettors can make bets almost immediately when new lines are posted by the sportsbooks. Often I hear of great bets made by the Las Vegas locals, but when I get there, the lines have already moved and are no longer as interesting. But there are things left over for people like me who do not live there, positive-EV futures among them.

NFL Futures

When people bet on NFL futures, they consider the strength of the team and the odds being offered. They weigh the two and if the odds offered are greater than their expectations, then they bet. This method makes sense, but it is not the best way.

You can do better by taking into consideration the expected market lines of games yet to be played. You can use expected market lines of future games to compare the futures bet to the combination of the individual money lines for the rest for of the season or playoffs. If the combination of the individual money lines offers better odds, then you are better off forgoing the futures bet and betting on each game as it comes up.

The advantages of using the expected market lines in games yet to be played are:

☐ You avoid making a futures bet that is inferior to betting multiple individual games

☐ You have a superior structure to value the ongoing risks of your bets

☐ You can figure out perfect hedge amounts in case you want to change positions

In chapter 8 the concept of predicting future lines was covered by looking at the whole NFL schedule before the season started. Here is an example of a NFC futures bet being analyzed late in the regular season.

2006 NFC Odds: Seattle

It is December 2006 and the Seahawks have clinched the NFC West. It looks like they will be slotted as the number four seed in the playoffs due to the records and tiebreakers of the division winners. In order to win the NFC, the Seahawks will need to win three playoff games. Their first playoff game will be at home against a wild-card team. Their second playoff game will be on the road against either the Bears or the Saints, the top two seeds. If the Seahawks make it to the NFC championship game, it will likely be on the road again, though they could get lucky and play at home against a wild-card team.

The best odds being offered in all the sportsbooks in Las Vegas on the Seahawks to win the NFC are 20-1. Here is my evaluation of the Seahawks to win the NFC by examining the expected line in each round of the playoffs.

Wild-card round

In the first playoff game, the Seahawks will play a wild-card team in Seattle. The Seahawks have a good home field advantage as their fans are vocal and supportive. The Seahawks are thought of as a team that was lucky to make the playoffs, and may have a worse W-L record than the wild-card team. Home playoff teams have done well historically; this fact may be built into the line. But the wild-card team they will face will likely be a better team. Even though the home-field advantage is worth roughly 3 points in the NFL, I am going to peg the Seahawks as a 2-point favorite, which is about 53% to win the game.

Divisional round

If the Seahawks win the first playoff game, then they will have to travel and play one of the teams that received a bye. Who they play depends on the outcome of the other NFC playoff game in round 1. There is a higher chance the Seahawks will play the number one seed, the Bears, who are considered the best team in the conference. Teams that get a bye in the first week are often big favorites at home in their first playoff game. Given that the Seahawks are thought to be a relatively weak team, and they will be playing the cream of the crop in the NFC, I peg the point spread at between 7 and 10 points. A 7 point underdog has about a 25% chance of winning the game, and a 10 point underdog has about a 20% chance of winning the game. I am going to use an average of these two percentages and go with 22.5%. This is a rough estimate, so I need to keep that in mind as part of my margin of error.

Conference finals

If the Seahawks win in round 2, they likely will travel again for the NFC conference title game. If they won as a big dog in round 2, the game was likely close rather than a blowout. They may not be as big an underdog in the NFC title game because they likely are playing a weaker team than they beat in round 2. Winning in round 2 may have increased their respect in the marketplace. There is also the remote chance that a wild-card team will get to the NFC conference title game, in which case the Seahawks would play at home, and would likely be the favorite. Given these assumptions, I am going to peg the chances of the Seahawks winning the NFC conference title game at 25%. This is another rough estimate. There are a lot of things that can happen between now and the NFC conference title game to change the odds. There is also the assumption that there are no major injuries that changes the relative talent of the teams. These estimated lines are made with the thought that the actual lines will have an equal chance of being higher or lower.

Putting it together

Now I have the estimated probabilities for all three rounds. Given the estimates above, I can calculate the chance of the Seahawks winning the NFC.

Round 1 (vs. wild-card team): 53%
Round 2 (vs. #1 or #2 seed): 22.5%
Round 3 (NFC Conference Final): 25%
Round 1 x Round 2 x Round 3 = Seahawk's probability to win the NFC
53% x 22.5% x 25% = 3% or 32-1.

The best line in Las Vegas is 20-1. Given the analysis above, 20-1 is a bad bet. Even though the Seahawks have already clinched a playoff berth and are one of six teams that can win the NFC, they are a long shot to get to the Super Bowl. That is because the Seahawks are likely to play two games on the road as big underdogs, and their likely lone home game is close to a coin flip.

The lines above reflect my estimates on the market lines in the future. But I thought the Seahawks were an underrated team. They had early-season injuries, but key components of their team would be ready for the playoffs. They would be a stronger team in the playoffs than they have shown in the regular season. Instead of market estimates of 53%, 22.5% and 25% in their possible three playoff games, suppose I think better estimates are 60%, 30% and 35%. Those odds indicate the Seahawks have a 6.3% chance (15-1) of winning the NFC. With these odds, betting the Seahawks to win the NFC at 20-1 looks to have positive EV.

However, even if I am right in handicapping that the Seahawks are a better team than the expected lines are implying, I would not bet them at 20-1. It does have positive EV assuming my handicapping is good, but there is more EV in waiting and betting on the Seahawks on each individual game. If my estimates for the expected lines are correct, then I can bet the Seahawks at a price close to 32-1 to win the NFC by betting them in the money line during each individual game. 32-1 is better than 20-1.

Of course I need to be comfortable with my estimates. They are rough, so I may go back and adjust the expected lines to make sure I am comfortable that I can get better value by betting them in individual games rather than the futures bet of 20-1.

This process is made more efficient when you go through it for every team that has a chance to make the playoffs. The sum of the probabilities for all the teams to win the NFC should be 100%. If you are expecting the Seahawks to have a 53% chance to beat the wild-card team in the first round, then you should be expecting the wild-card team to have a 47% chance to beat the Seahawks. If you change the expected line of one team in a specific game in the playoffs, you need to adjust the expected line on their potential opponents. Thus changing the line for one team to get a new estimate on futures odds for that team will affect your estimates of futures odds for other teams as well. The NFL playoffs are a zero-sum game. Only one team can win the NFC.

Tiebreakers

A sportsbook can overlook a tiebreaker situation and put up a beatable line.

College football

College football teams do not play many games within their conference. It is not unusual for teams to share the same record atop the conference at the end of the year. Tiebreaker rules come into play to decide the conference winner or, in the case of conferences that have divisions, the team that plays in the conference title game. Typically, the first tiebreaker is the head-to-head game. But sometimes the teams do not play each other that year or there are more than two teams tied. When betting on conference futures in college football in the middle of the season, you should understand the tiebreaker rules and know which team holds the advantage.

Here is an example from the PAC-10 in 2006. The conference winner would be determined by the outcome of the game between California and USC on November 18. This was the case despite the fact that both still had one more PAC-10 game left in their schedule, and USC had another non-conference game left: Notre Dame.

Both teams were 6-1 going into this game. Whoever won the game would hold the tiebreaker advantage and for the purposes of the conference title, it would not have mattered what happened in their last conference game of the year. At worst, the winning team in this game would have gone 7-2 (if it lost the last game of the year). At best, the losing team would have gone 7-2 as well (if it won the last game of the year). But the winning team in the USC-California game would have the tiebreaker advantage. Given the tiebreaker situation, the PAC-10 conference odds should have been the same as the money line in this particular game. A sportsbook might make the mistake of thinking the last game of the year matters in the conference standings. With this incorrect thinking, they may put up juicy conference futures odds.

The point spread in the game was USC -6; in college football, that corresponds to a money line of -205. I was lucky to find a sportsbook offering California +230 to win the PAC-10. That same sportsbook offered USC -220 to win the game. I bet California to win the PAC-10 at +230 and did not hedge. My wager lost as USC won the game and the PAC-10.

NFL

NFL divisional futures have this dynamic as well, but are more complicated. Unlike college football where the teams play each other once a year during the regular season, NFL teams play the other teams in the same division twice a year. Two teams can be tied for the division with each having won one game. They must go farther into a list of tiebreaker rules in order to decide the division winner. NFL.com has the current tiebreaker rules. This is important for division futures, conference futures, and Super Bowl futures. If two teams are tied atop a division, the team that wins the division may get a bye in the first round of the playoffs while the other team may be a wild-card team and have to play on the road in the first round. One team has to win two games, of which at least one will be at home, to make it to the Super Bowl. The other team has to win three games to make it to the Super Bowl, and probably all three games will be on the road.

Late in the season, NFL futures bettors need to examine the tiebreaker rules and carefully adjust their futures calculations to account for tiebreaker advantages or disadvantages. Not knowing the rules can result in incorrect calculations and negative-EV bets. Sometimes NFL tiebreaker scenarios are complex, with the result hinging on multiple games. With hard work, you may be able to take advantage of these situations.

MLB: Wild-Card Race

When you make a futures bet, you usually are rooting for your team to win as many games as possible. The more games your team wins, the better it is for your wager. But there is one futures bet where you are hoping your team does well, but not too well. If your team does too well, then you may lose your bet. This futures bet is on the wild-card race in baseball.

In early August 2005 I noticed something interesting while running simulations to create probabilistic estimates on the wild-card winners in baseball. Three teams were tied for the wild card spot: the Yankees (NYY), the Athletics (OAK) and the Indians (CLE). The simulations estimated their final records as:

Team	Expected Wins
NYY	90.2
CLE	89.4
OAK	88.3

I thought OAK was a better team than CLE. If the season started on that day, I would expect OAK to win 81.7 games and CLE to win 81.1 games. In my opinion they had both outperformed their true talent; thus they were on pace to win many more games than their talent would predict. I expected CLE to win more games for the remainder of 2005 due to an easier schedule of remaining games.

Based on the expected season wins, you might think that NYY had the best chance at being the wild card. That was not the case. Here are the estimates for each team being the wild card.

Team	Wild-Card Probability
NYY	29.4%
CLE	36.9%
OAK	10.4%
BOS	10.3%
MIN	5.9%
LAA	4.8%
CHW	1.9%

Although I had NYY expected to win more games than CLE, I had CLE with the best chance of being the wild card because the wild-card team must finish second in its division, not first. NYY had a good chance of winning its division. CLE had a low chance of winning its division because the Chicago White Sox (CHW) had a big lead. Playing better gives a team a better shot at being the wild card, up to a point. Playing great reduces a team's chances of being the wild card by increasing its chances of winning its division. Here are the estimates for each wild card hopeful to win its division.

Team	Division Probability
NYY	25.9%
CLE	2.8%
OAK	28.7%

CLE had a low chance of winning its division. Even if it played great, the best it could realistically hope for is to be the wild card. CHW simply had too large a lead. NYY and OAK were different. If they played great the rest of the season, they had realistic chances of winning their divisions.

This is why my simulations estimated CLE as the front-runner for the wild card at 36.9%. If you look just at team strength, my conclusion does not make sense in that I have CLE rated below NYY in terms of expected wins for the season, and I also have CLE rated below OAK in terms of overall talent. But for being the wild card, CLE has two advantages: a low chance of winning its division and an easy schedule.

Head to Head Down the Stretch

Near the end of the season, teams behind in the standings greatly value head-to-head games against teams ahead of them. Those games are important because a win also means a loss for the team ahead.

Suppose the Astros are two games behind the Cardinals with two games left. In one scenario they play each other; in another scenario they play different teams. Assume if they play each other, the money line would be +100 (50%) for each game; but if they play other teams, the Astros and Cards would each would be -122 (55%) favorites in each of their games. In order for the Astros to have a chance, they need to win both of their games and they also need the Cardinals to lose both of their games. If that occurs, then they play a one-game playoff to decide the division.

If the Astros play the Cardinals in the last two games of the season, they have a 25% chance of tying the Cardinals and forcing a one-game playoff for the division. That gives them a 12.5% chance of winning the division.

Astros win both games = 50% x 50% = 25%
Astros play and beat Cardinals in one-game playoff = 25% x 50% = 12.5%

If the Astros and the Cardinals play different teams, the Astros have a 6.1% chance of tying the Cardinals and forcing a one-game playoff for the division. That gives them a 3.1% chance of winning the division.

Astros win both games = 55% x 55% = 30.25%
Cardinals lose both games = 45% x 45% = 20.25%
Astros play and beat Cardinals in one-game playoff = 30.25% x 20.25% x 50% = 3.1%

An interesting note is that in the scenario when the Astros play the Cardinals, they actually expect to win fewer games within the 162-game regular season even though they have higher chance of winning the division. They expect to win 1 (.5 + .5) game in the next two against the Cardinals. (I am not counting the possibility of a win in the playoff game because some sportsbooks will not count that in the regular season wins wager.) If they do not play the Cardinals, the Astos expect to win 1.1 games (.55 + .55). Normally a higher number of wins means a higher chance of winning the division. But in this case, the head-to-head games have more value for the Astros.

CHAPTER 19
TIPS FOR
HANDICAPPERS

Be Ready for Opening Lines

There is an explanation of how lines open in Chapter 4. A fresh line hung by an aggressive sportsbook reflects the opinions of only a few people. An early line is often not an efficient number. Line makers can make mistakes. If the market disagrees with the line makers' opinion, then betting action will favor one team and lines will move. Closing lines often differ from opening lines. Most line movement comes early, as the sharp bettors make their bets and the sportsbooks adjust.

If you are ready to bet opening numbers, you will be able to take advantage of weak early lines before other sharp handicappers do. If you are slow, then the line may have adjusted to a more efficient number by the time you are ready to bet, and you will have missed an opportunity. Thus it is a good idea to handicap games as early as possible, preferably before the lines come out. If you have handicapped the lines before the sportsbooks put up theirs, you will be able to take advantage of their mistakes.

In sports that are played daily, aggressive sportsbooks put up lines the day before the event. These are called overnight lines. In football, sportsbooks put up early lines on Sunday night, around the time of the weekly Sunday night football game. The limits on early lines are smaller than usual and smaller bets are more likely to move early lines. There are two reasons why sportsbooks do this:

☐   Squares don't bet early lines; sharps do.

☐   Sportsbooks are less comfortable with their early lines because they realize they may have made mistakes.

The people who are betting early lines are more knowledgeable about betting their sport. They are already thinking ahead to the next game, often betting tomorrow's games before today's games are played. They are more likely to be winning bettors than random people making bets five minutes before game time. Thus sportsbooks are more careful taking these bets and give more respect to early action, especially if it comes from known sharp bettors.

Lines Getting Sharper

The betting lines in the last few years have gotten sharper, most noticeably in the NFL. As more and more educated and sharp players have entered the market, sportsbooks have adjusted. Lines are tighter and it is tougher to win money. This is the thought of many sharp players who have been around a few years. Here is an example of a game line that would have been surprising a few years back.

It is early in the 2005 NFL season. The Oakland Raiders had a 4-12 record in 2003 and a 5-12 record in 2004. They started off the 2005 season with three straight losses, covering the spread only once. The Cowboys made the playoffs in 2003, had a poor year in 2004, and are 2-1 in 2005. The general perception is that the Cowboys, with Bill Parcells as head coach, have a shot at making the playoffs.

In the fourth week of the 2005 season, the Cowboys are playing at Oakland. What do you think the line should be? Based on the records, it seems that the Cowboys should be considered the better team. Yet the line on the game was Raiders -3. With a typical home field advantage of 3 points in the NFL, this line reflects that the market thinks the two teams are equal in this game. I believe in the same situation in past years, the line would have been around even money.

The line makers have adjusted to smarter bettors. In recent years the line seems to have done a better job of recognizing "must win" situations. This game could break the Raiders' season. If they lose, they will be 0-4 and their season will appear hopeless. The Raider players know this, and are giving maximum focus and effort in preparation for the game. The Raiders may be a worse team than the Cowboys, but the difference is not that great. Superior motivation for the Raiders in this game is enough to project them to a 3 point favorite.

The Raiders won the game 19-13, but they finished the year with a 4-12 record. The Cowboys missed the playoffs with a 9-7 record.

Be flexible. Good opportunities in sports betting will disappear sooner or later. You can not count on using the same old handicapping angles year after year. Every year some opportunities disappear, and you have to find new ones.

Angles

There are many angles in sports betting. Bettors find these angles and sometimes bet them blindly. But without the knowledge of the line's starting base, how do you know if the angle is already built into the line? The sports-betting marketplace is fairly efficient, and it learns from the past. It is possible that a successful angle from the past is now known to other sports bettors and line makers. If the impact of the angle is already built into lines, then there is no value in blindly betting the angle. To find out if an angle still has value, you need to figure out what the line should be in the absence of the angle. The question you should be asking is: "What should the line be if the angle were not relevant?" Methods that can help in answering that question come from handicapping and other forms of line analysis. Without an idea of the starting base, you will not know if there is value in the angle. Here are a couple of examples.

College football: returning starters

Angle

The number of returning starters on a college football team is a common statistic that bettors analyze early in a new season. Teams with a high number of returning starters have players who know their teammates well and have experience with the playbook and the style of play employed by the coaches. Teams with a low number of returning starters do not enjoy this advantage.

In the first and second games of the season, if there is a large difference in the number of returning starters, the team with the higher number of returning starters has an advantage. You may add some twists, such as giving more credit for a returning starting quarterback and passing on teams with new head coaches.

Starting base and current line

The problem with blindly betting on the number of returning starters is the possibility that the market has already adjusted for the angle. It is possible the angle was a winner in the past, but line makers and bettors learned about the angle and adjusted the lines accordingly. Similar match-ups in today's market may have different lines relative to markets from years past. If you do not know the level of the starting base without the impact of the angle, then you will have a tough time figuring out whether or not the angle is already built into the line.

Betting the angle

If you have the ability to handicap starting base lines, then you can figure out whether the angle is built into the line. With a good starting base line, you can see if it is still worthwhile to make a bet based on the angle. The sports-betting market learns fast. If you have found a way to make money, other bettors may be looking at the same thing. Line makers catch up too, and that is how sports betting lines become efficient, thus rendering some angles irrelevant.

Baseball angle: sign-stealing

Angle

Suppose a MLB team catches your attention with its outstanding hitting during home day games, game after game. You suspect something is up; perhaps the team is stealing its opponent's pitch selection signs and relaying them to the hitter before the pitch is thrown.

Starting base and current line

Under normal circumstances, switching ballparks causes a 40-cent swing in the odds. For example, a team that is a -140 favorite at home would be about even money if the same two pitchers face either other at the other ballpark, assuming unchanged expectations about either team.

That expected 40-cent swing in the odds can give you a handle on whether the extra hit production you have noticed has been factored into the line on today's game. Look over the records of past games to find the most recent game in which today's pitchers faced each other in the other ballpark. If the line on today's game is 40 cents more in favor of today's home team, you can conclude that the line maker has not factored in the extra offensive power you have noticed.

Use Statistics in Context

Statistics should be used in context of the teams, players and game situations; sometimes they can be misleading. Rushing yards for a running quarterback can be one of these misleading statistics. Here is a hypothetical example of a handicapper looking at the Falcons.

Yards per carry is a key statistic in the NFL. A favorite angle is to bet on an underdog that outrushes its opponents in yards per carry. As you are looking through the statistics, you find a game that fits this angle. The Falcons are a 5-point road underdog to the Patriots. In yards per carry, the Falcons are ahead of the Patriots by 4.1 yards to 4.0. You decide to bet on the Falcons since they fit your angle.

While it is true that the Falcons out-rushed the Patriots by a little, are there mitigating factors that change the way the statistics look? If you dig deeper into the details, you would find that the statistical advantage that the Falcons hold in rushing the ball may be due to the fact they are so poor at passing the ball. Michael Vick is great running the ball, but he is not an accurate passer. Too often he runs the ball instead of throwing it. While Vick may gain yards on the ground and make the rushing statistics for the Falcons look good, he is doing it at the expense of the passing game. Another quarterback in his place won't run for 80 yards per game; instead, the other quarterback may pass for 125 more yards than Vick. Instead of completing a 15 yard pass when it is third down and 14 yards to go, Vick is scrambling and gaining 8 yards, enhancing the rushing statistics but falling short of the first down. Thus the rushing statistics for the Falcons are deceiving; their rushing numbers should be viewed differently due to their unusual quarterback talent. Going into the details of what the numbers represents allows you to understand that this is not a normal case for this specific angle. Now that you know the details, you can make a better assessment of whether you want to bet this angle in this game.

Weed out the Luck

Randomness and luck play a big part of outcomes of team sports. Such sayings as "baseball is a game of inches" and "footballs bounce in strange ways" reflect how luck can play a big part in the final scores of games. Handicappers should try to weed out the luck out of past results and focus on statistics that reflect true ability rather than luck. Handicappers that are able to do this have a better chance of succeeding. Here is an example in baseball.

Sabremetrics is the science of understanding baseball through statistics. More than any other sport, people love to dive into baseball statistics to glean the truth. Over time, research has shown that some popular statistics have a high degree of luck associated with them. A pitcher's win-loss record is one of those statistics. A pitcher's win-loss record reflects not only his performance, but also the performance of the fielders and hitters on his team. If he pitches great, but his team does not score any runs, he can't win the game. If he gives up 5 runs while his team scores 6, he gets the win, but, it was luck. The media rely too much on a pitcher's win-loss record when deciding their Cy Young Award votes. Good handicappers have the ability to weed out the luck from past results.

One Sport at a Time

If you are inexperienced as a handicapper, concentrate on one sport at a time. Handicapping any sport successfully is difficult and time consuming. Trying to handicap two sports at the same time means you have to divide your focus and energy between the sports. That could lead to less than optimal performance in either or both sports. Even those handicappers who do beat widely available lines do so by only a small margin. For example, a 2% decrease in expected performance can turn a winning handicapper who expects to beat widely available lines at a 54% clip into a break-even handicapper at 52%. It is better to beat one sport by a small margin than to be a break-even handicapper in multiple sports.

Here are some advantages that handicappers have if they focus on just one sport.

News

It is vital to follow the news about injuries, players and coaches. There is a lot of news nowadays with all the media coverage and you can easily fill your time keeping up to date with the news on one sport. Following two sports means less attention paid to any one sport, and that could mean missing a small but important bit of news.

Relative-value plays

Handicapping should not be about individual games only. There are other types of bets put up by sportsbooks. A lot of the information needed to evaluate individual games can be used for other types of bets. You should be able to use your skills in handicapping individual games to find value in some futures, props and other relative-value plays as well.

Market moves and tendencies

Betting markets and line moves sometimes have tendencies that you may be able to anticipate. Focusing on one sport at a time allows you maximum time to watch line movements and try to keep track of market activity. You ought to turn your opinions into wagers at some point, so you need to keep track of how the lines move. For example, if the market on many games is known to move at a certain time each week due to the released plays by another handicapper, then that is crucial information for everyone. If you feel you are probably going to have the same opinions as the other handicapper, and his released plays move the lines drastically, then you need to make your bets before he releases.

Choose a Sport You Like

Choose a sport you enjoy. The enjoyment level may come from playing the game, watching the games on TV or in person, thinking about the game, reading about the game or other reasons. If you are not interested in a sport you are handicapping, you are more apt to miss pertinent information. Handicapping will feel more like a job. The more you enjoy your handicapping, the more successful you are at it.

Being interested in the sport is important because you will be focused on following all the news and nuances of the sport. Throughout any season (and the off-season as well), players and teams will go through changes that you need to be aware of in order to adjust your numbers correctly. These include: injuries, player improvement or decline, position changes, coaching adjustments, the market's changing perception on a certain team or player and many other things. If you are not interested in following the sport, you are more likely to miss important changes to a team's strength and quality. But if you are interested in following the sport, you will be eager to gobble up any information you can get.

Most winning sports bettors can be successful in other fields. Even if they can make more money doing something else, many winning sports bettors choose to bet sports because they get more enjoyment out of sports betting. In other words, for many successful sports bettors, the EV of a career in sports betting is less than the EV of a career in the corporate world; but the expected utility (EU) is higher for them in sports betting because of the quality of life. EU is an individual preference. Different people enjoy different things. Some people do not enjoy sports or gambling, others love it. This is why I think it is important for handicappers to choose sports that they enjoy. It is possible for a handicapper to think that he has more edge against the sportsbooks in sports that he may be less interested in, but if he does not enjoy those sports, then there is no real difference between handicapping those sports and analyzing stocks for a Wall Street firm.

CHAPTER 20 TIPS FOR BETTORS

You can make money with or without handicapping. You must be knowledgeable about the value of different points in the sports you bet. You must work to find the best numbers and the best opportunities. This chapter contains some tips and thoughts for you to improve your game.

Shop

Shopping for the best line is crucial to success. The difference between getting an extra half point versus the widely available lines may not seem important because it will not come into play for most games. But there are enough games where the extra half point matters. In the long run, those half points add up. Getting a better price on the money line or lower juice on the point spread can be just as valuable. If you can get a line at one sportsbook at a half point better than at another sportsbook (with the same juice on both bets), then you can turn a possible push into a win and a possible loss into a push. The game may not land on the exact number that often, but over hundreds of bets it will happen enough to become important.

Here is an example of how much you can increase your yearly winnings if you can get an extra half point on 10% of your bets.

Suppose you make 3,000 bets a year on basketball games, risking $110 per game at -110. You will put a total of $330,000 into action for the year.

If you work hard and shop around for the best lines, you can expect to get an extra half point (at the same juice) on 10% of your bets. If you are making 3,000 bets a year, you can get an extra half point on 300 bets.

Roughly 3.3% of basketball games land on each number that is close to the point spread. For example, for a line of +4.5, there is a 3.3% chance of the actual game difference landing on +4 and a 3.3% chance of the actual game difference landing on +5. If you get an extra half point on 300 games, the expectation is that 10 games will turn from a losing bet into a push or from a push into a winner.

For $110 bets, 10 games changing from losers to pushes or pushes to winners increases your win for the year by $1000 to $1100. If you are a 54% handicapper making 3,000 bets per year, that can mean increasing your earnings by 10%.

Finding a Sportsbook

An important aspect of sports betting is finding a place to make your wagers. The lines or the wagers that the sportsbook is willing to take can trump all other aspects of sports betting. It may not matter how much you know or how well you handicap. If you cannot place a bet at a good price, then you cannot turn your great ideas into money. This is similar to a great blackjack counter being barred from playing blackjack at many casinos; he cannot turn his knowledge into money as easily anymore. Here are a couple of sports betting examples.

NFL teaser example

You like playing NFL two team six-point teasers. These bets have good value under the right circumstances and the right lines. (See Stanford Wong's *Sharp Sports Betting* for more information on NFL teasers.) The edge in teasers depends heavily on the juice that you have to lay with the sportsbook. In Las Vegas, it is tough to find sportsbooks that will take two-team teasers at -110 anymore. With a line of -120, two-team six-point teasers are not nearly as attractive. A sportsbook willing to take these at +100 or -110 is a valuable asset as those lines allow you to make many positive-EV bets throughout the season. Finding sportsbooks that offer the nice prices is just as valuable as understanding which wagers have positive EV. Without a place to make your bet, you cannot execute your knowledge.

NFL futures example

Most Las Vegas sportsbooks inject a substantial amount of juice into their futures odds. If you convert the odds for all the teams into percentages, and add them up, you would get 100% if there were no house edge. Understandably the sportsbooks need an edge, so the sum will be more than 100%. The problem is that too many sportsbooks have futures odds that add up to a ridiculous amount, sometimes approaching 200%. In that unfriendly betting atmosphere, it is tough to find any value in futures.

A sportsbook that has a combined 125% on futures can be valuable. Knowing which sportsbooks are friendly means you can save time by visiting only them, and avoiding the unfriendly sportsbooks. For example, in Las Vegas I have learned not to bother spending any time checking Harrah's futures numbers. The markup is way too high, and the limits way too low. Why bother wasting time in their properties? On the other hand, there are a handful of casinos I will visit every time I go to Las Vegas, just to see their futures lines.

College football correlated parlay

Sometimes two sport bets will have a connection to each other. If one event happens, then another event is more likely than usual to happen. When that situation occurs, the two bets are said to be positively correlated. Here is an example.

In college football, powerhouse Nebraska is playing against a small school. The small school has no chance of winning, and has little chance of even scoring in the game. The point spread in the game is Nebraska -50 and the total is 53. Each of the bets may have a 50% chance of winning, but if one wins, the other is highly likely to win as well. If Nebraska covers the 50 points, the game is likely to go over 53. Thus Nebraska in the point spread and the over in the total are correlated. Likewise the small school and the under are correlated.

If you find a sportsbook stupid enough to offer regular parlay odds on correlated parlays, then you have found a gold mine. Regular parlay odds are 13 to 5, which is equivalent to 27.8%. It is rare to find anyone willing to let you bet obviously correlated parlays like the Nebraska/over example. The good news is there are other events that are related in subtle ways. The events have a connection where if one bet wins, then the other bet is more likely to win. The connection may not be as strong as the example used here, but as long as it is strong enough to beat 13 to 5 odds, then you have a positive-EV situation.

The Best Time to Bet

Even though you should handicap games early before lines come out (as discussed in the previous chapter), it does not necessarily mean that you should bet games early. The timing of placing the bets depends on these issues.

☐ How big do you bet?

☐ How do you think the line will move?

☐ How sharp do you think the market is in this sport?

How big do you bet?

If you bet bigger than the maximum limits when the early line opens, then it may be prudent to wait until more sportsbooks have put up their lines. Typically, sportsbooks have smaller limits on the lines they put up early. This includes overnights, which are lines they put up the night before the game on sports that are played daily: basketball, baseball and hockey. Sportsbooks are more eager to adjust their lines based on small wagers in the overnight market than they normally would. If you bet early, then other sportsbooks may copy the adjusted line that is later posted by the sportsbook where you made the wager.

For example, let's say you want to bet $5,000 on under 185 in a college basketball total between Sacramento State and Idaho State. The maximum limit in the early line may be $500 even if the normal limit on game day is $5,000. The overnight line comes out at 185 and you bet $500 on the under at Sportsbook A. Since it is an overnight line, Sportsbook A has lower limits and is more willing to move the line due to action since it normally gets action from sharper players on its overnight lines. It may also factor in who is making the bet and how much the sportsbook respects the bettor's opinion. Sportsbook A decides to move the total down to 184 based on your bet. When the other sportsbooks put up their lines the next morning, they also have 184 instead of 185. You are not sure if the other sportsbooks looked at Sportsbook A's lines and put up 184. Maybe they would have put up a total of 185 if the line at Sportsbook A was still 185. You no longer have the chance to bet under 185, and all you got was a $500 bet. You start to wonder if you had not bet the $500 on the overnight line at Sportsbook A, then maybe there would have been a better chance of getting to bet $5,000 on under 185 once all the sportsbooks open their lines. On the other hand, it is also possible that if you did not make any bets on the overnight line, the line still would have gone down to 184. That would be worse as you would not get even $500 into action. If your bet size is $5,000, then increasing the chance to bet $5,000 may be worth the risk of losing the chance to make a $500 bet.

If you bet less than the maximum limits when the early line opens, then your best alternative is to bet early, especially if you are on the right side and the line will move even if you don't make the wager. Early lines are typically softer than later lines. If you are a good handicapper (or are following a good handicapper), then the line is more likely to move if the sportsbook puts up a line that disagrees with your number. So it seems advantageous to bet early and get a good line rather than wait and see a more efficient line later.

How do you think the line will move?

If you are confident the line will move in the same direction as your opinion, then you want to bet as early as possible. If you think the line may move in the other direction, then it is best to wait until it does move. This skill of predicting line movement is different than the skill of handicapping. It takes knowledge of the marketplace and how other people think about the teams and the line.

For example, I thought the fair line in game 7 of the 2003 ALCS was the Red Sox -140 at the Yankees, with Pedro Martinez versus Roger Clemens. After the conclusion of game 6, the overnight line opened as Red Sox -120. I refrained from betting into the overnight line because I expected heavy action from Yankee fans to move the line down. Before 2004 the Yankees always seemed to get the best of the Red Sox and beat them at every turn. Even though Martinez was a superior pitcher to Clemens at this stage in their careers, the Yankee mystique meant there would be lots of people betting on the Yankees if they were an underdog, especially at home. Even though I thought the Red Sox -120 was a positive-EV bet, I got a better price by waiting until after Yankee backers made their bets. I lost the bet as the Yankees won Game 7 on a dramatic home run by Aaron Boone in extra innings.

How sharp do you think the market is?

If the market is sharp in the sport you are handicapping, then any bad line will move quickly to a more efficient line. In an efficient sports betting market, if there is any edge, bettors should jump on it and be happy with it. Waiting means other sharp players will jump on the bad line and you will miss your opportunity.

If the market is not as sharp in your sport, then you have more leeway in waiting until the time is right. This may mean waiting until more sportsbooks have put up lines so you can bet as big as you want. Or it could mean waiting because you believe the square public money is going to move the line, giving you a better price later on.

Win Big or Slowly?

In the summer of 2006 I found a sportsbook offering an interesting prop on all baseball games. My research told me that I had a 10% edge on that prop on an average of three games per day. My method of handicapping the prop was superior to the method the sportsbook used to set its lines. Such opportunities are fleeting.

If my personal risk parameters permit me to make bets that are considerably less than the sportsbooks' limit, then I can bet my own maximum without worrying about the sportsbook noticing. But if my personal risk parameters permit me to bet at the sportsbooks' max, then it is useful to think about the best way to maximize EV. That was the case for me with these props. Should I bet the max, or something less than the max?

Bet the max, and hope they don't notice

The advantage of this approach is that I could get the most EV out of each game where the line was off. Betting less would be leaving positive EV uncollected on any individual game.

The disadvantage of this approach is if my bets bring attention to the prop, the sportsbook might modify the way it sets the lines, and it would not take much adjustment for my betting profit to disappear.

Bet smaller, and hope they don't adjust

The alternative to betting the maximum is to bet a smaller amount. Taking this approach might reduce the chance the sportsbook rethinks its lines. Smaller wagers have a smaller chance of being noticed. Even if my wagers mostly win, the wins might fly below the radar. The advantage of betting smaller is it increases the chance of staying in action and continuing to bet. The hope of this approach is that in the long run, the cumulative smaller bets will have more EV than a smaller number of bigger bets. The disadvantage is that if the sportsbook does not mind the big bets and does not change its lines even if I am winning with big bets, then I have passed up some EV.

There is another possibility: the chance that another big bettor sees the same opportunity and makes the same bets I am making. If that happens, then the benefits of betting small no longer exist, as the sportsbook is likely to notice the combined wagers. Given this possibility, I decided to bet the maximum. By early 2007 the sportsbook had adjusted: I was finding only one bet per day, and that bet promised only a 5% edge.

Traps

There are traps that all bettors can fall into, including successful bettors. You should continue to work hard and advance your knowledge. Here are some possible traps to avoid.

Forgetting the value of money

If you are playing 100-200 Texas Hold'em and have swings of $2,000 to $10,000 a day, after a while you might forget what $100 means in the real world. You think of $100 as a small blind, thus no big deal. Soon you may not bat an eye at spending $100 at lunch. Instead of walking when time is not of the essence, a $20 cab ride now seems like a cheap way to get down the Strip. A $4,000 Rolex watch does not seem like a big deal after a $20,000 score. These are lifestyle expenses of a gambler that can never be recouped.

If you make your money as salary, you do not get paid in cash on a daily basis, and you do not carry around a huge bankroll. You don't have the same perception problems about money that gamblers do. The cash that a gambler carries around should not be viewed as spending cash, but rather as tools for his trade.

Disdain for small bets

Why bother shopping to find the best line on a $300 bet with 10 cents of edge when you are betting $2,000 on other games? Those $300 bets seem meaningless in comparison, but they are important if there are enough of them. Forgoing those wagers means the negative swings will hurt more.

Resting on your laurels

Bookmakers and line makers are smart. Other players are smart too. If you use the same strategies year after year, and never adapt or pick up new strategies, your strategies will start to lose their edge over the sportsbooks. Sportsbooks may adapt enough that you no longer have an edge. Or they may even stop taking the type of bets you have learned to beat. You need to continue to find new opportunities.

Not admitting mistakes

Successful bettors think they are smart, and they probably are. But they can make mistakes too. If a successful bettor gets too big of an ego, he may not see his own mistakes and admit to them. It is better to admit a mistake and learn from it, than to lose more money due to stubbornness.

CHAPTER 21 HANDICAPPERS

Wagering on the picks of another handicapper is known as following the handicapper. If you are going to do that, you need to handicap the handicappers and determine who is worthwhile to follow. In this chapter, I will set forth some guidelines on how to evaluate handicappers.

Following a Handicapper

Here are some possible reasons why you might be willing to follow another handicapper's picks:

☐ You do not have confidence in your own handicapping and are looking for a talented handicapper to provide positive-EV picks.

☐ Even if you are a positive-EV handicapper, you believe the other handicapper will come up with positive-EV plays that are different from your own. This adds another set of positive-EV plays that you would not have otherwise played.

☐ To improve your own handicapping by learning from other handicappers

☐ To get a jump on line moves for scalping and middling purposes

These are valid reasons to follow a handicapper. But that does not mean you should expect to make money by following just any handicapper. Some handicappers give out positive-EV plays, but others give out negative-EV plays, though not on purpose. You want a handicapper to provide more EV than the cost of the picks. Few handicappers produce profits for their followers. Even well-known touts who have been in the business a long time may not truly be winners; it may be a mirage of marketing, showmanship, and luck. Handicapping a handicapper is crucial if you want to put your money on his opinions.

A Handicapper's Record

A handicapper's record is often expressed as a percentage. But that number alone does not tell the whole story; in fact, it may be misleading. Here are some issues to consider when evaluating a handicapper's record.

Sample size

The sample size is important. When a tout shouts that he won 80% of his last 10 games, that is useless information since luck is the dominant factor in such a small sample size. Anyone can go on a short-term hot streak. Surely those 10 games are not the only games the handicapper has picked in his life. Why is he not including the pick he made eleven games ago? I guarantee you that 11th pick was a loser! If it had been a winner, then the tout would be claiming he was 9-2 in his last 11 picks, and using 81.8% as his winning percentage.

You do not want to bet a handicapper's picks if you think he was merely lucky. A good record with a small sample of picks probably came from good luck alone. To help evaluate a handicapper's record given the sample size, you can use the binomial distribution formula. The formula gives the probability a handicapper wins fewer games than a set number given the number of overall picks and an expected true winning percentage. This formula requires you assume an expected true winning percentage for the handicapper prior. Since point spread lines usually require the bettor to lay -110 vig, a common number to use initially in the formula is 52.4%. If the result of the binomial distribution formula shows the handicapper had a high chance of accumulating fewer wins than he actually did, then that may be used as evidence that the assumption that he is a 52.4% handicapper is too low.

The formula in Microsoft Excel is:

=BINOMDIST(X,Y,Z,TRUE)
X is the number of wins
Y is the number of picks
Z is the expected true winning percentage.

The result is the probability that a handicapper picked at random accumulates X or fewer wins over Y picks given he has an expected true winning percentage of Z%.

For example, suppose a handicapper has gone 165-135. Assuming he is a break-even handicapper against -110 lines, you can find the probability that he accumulates 165 or fewer wins over 300 picks. 11/21 or 52.4% is the break-even point against -110 lines.

=BINOMDIST(165,300,11/21,TRUE)
= 83.3%

The 52.4% handicapper has an 83.3% chance of winning 165 or fewer games over any 300 game stretch. Given such a high rate, it is natural to wonder whether the true winning percentage of the 165-135 handicapper is higher than 52.4%. This formula does not give you that answer, but it can act as supporting evidence.

The following table below shows handicappers who picked 54% winners over various amount of picks. The results show the chance the handicapper accumulates at most the number of wins listed over the number of picks assuming his expected true winning percentage is 52.4%.

Wins	27	54	108	216	432
Picks	50	100	200	400	800
Probability	64.4%	66.4%	70.1%	75.7%	83.0%

With 50 picks, there is a 64.4% chance of accumulating 27 or fewer wins. With more picks at the same winning percentage, the probability the handicapper accumulated fewer than the listed number of picks increases. With 800 picks, the result is 83%. Bigger sample size gives you more confidence luck was less of a factor.

This formula can be useful, but keep in mind that you can be misled even with this seemingly objective evaluation. For example, you may have only partial data for the handicapper. A handicapper may have picked 165 winners out of 300 games in one year; but there may be more picks that you are ignoring or are unaware of. Maybe the handicapper picked 150 winners in 300 games the previous season. If that is the case, then the cumulative record is 315 wins out of 600 games, and the result using the Excel formula would be 53.9%, which is lower than 83.3%.

Lines the handicapper used

You must be able to find the same lines a handicapper uses to grade his picks. The concept of "widely available lines" comes into play here. Widely available means the line is easy for you to find and bet. If a handicapper uses lines that you cannot find, then you have the choice of not betting or betting into a worse line. If you bet into a worse line than the handicapper used for his pick, then you should expect a lower winning percentage and lower ROI than the handicapper achieves. The differences in the lines might be enough to turn his winning record into a losing one for you.

Here is an example of betting into a worse line to your detriment. A 55% handicapper picks the NFL Falcons -3 -110, but you bet the Falcons at -3.5 -110. You just made a horrible bet even if the handicapper is expected to win at a 55% rate on his picks. When the point spread is 3 in the NFL, the game is expected to land exactly on that number about 10.2% of the time. Given the handicapper has a 55% chance of winning, here is the expected distribution as it pertains to the wager.

Handicapper Takes Falcons -3

Result	Incl Pushes	No Pushes
Falcons cover	49.4%	55.0%
Falcons win by 3	10.2%	
Falcons don't cover	40.4%	45.0%

Someone who bets the Falcons -3.5 is not participating in the same profit profile as the handicapper's suggested Falcons -3 pick. Falcons by 3 loses when the handicapper's pick pushed. Bettors of Falcons -3.5 should expect to win at a 49.4% rate, which is a negative-EV bet against a line with -110 juice.

Falcons Bet, Not Counting Pushes

	Falcons -3	Falcons -3.5
Win %	55.0%	49.4%
Lose %	45.0%	50.6%

The 3 is the number that lands the most often in the NFL. Other numbers land less often; therefore other half-point differences are less important. Some numbers occur so infrequently that you can take a worse line and still expect to have a good bet. Here is an example where a 55% handicapper releases a pick of Colts -12, but you can find only Colts -12.5. The 12 does not land often in the NFL, only about 0.6% of the time.

Colts Bet, Recognizing Pushes

Result	Colts -12	Colts -12.5
Colts cover	54.65%	55.0%
Colts win by 12	0.60%	
Colts don't cover	44.75%	45.0%

You should not expect to win at a 55% rate since you are taking a worse number than the line the handicapper used. Instead, you should expect a slightly lower win rate, 54.65% in this example. The difference is smaller in this example than the previous one. It is a positive-EV bet against a line with -110 juice.

Colts Bet, Not Counting Pushes

	Colts -12	Colts -12.5
Win %	55.0%	54.65%
Lose %	45.0%	45.35%

If you consider betting into a worse line than what the handicapper used for his pick, you must be aware of the value of each number, as shown in table 6 of chapter 9. Sometimes getting a worse line turns a positive-EV bet into a negative-EV bet; and sometimes the bet is still positive EV.

Handicappers selling multiple services

It is not cause for alarm when handicappers separate their picks by sport. However, multiple categories of picks in the same sport are used specifically to fool potential customers. Even if the handicapper is no better than a coin flipper, at least one of his categories ought to show good results due to randomness and small sample sizes. For example, a handicapper may have the following records in four different services:

Executive:	10-15
Premier:	15-10
First Class:	9-16
Gold:	16-9

The combined record is 50-50. Yet this handicapper will likely market the Premier Level and the Gold Level, 15-10 and 16-9 respectively; and ignore the losing services. The winning records look legitimate but they are misleading; they do not capture the whole picture.

Even some solid handicappers use this trickery to entice clients to pay for their services. Solid handicappers should eschew such trickery, as customers will stick with them in the long run if they are truly winning handicappers.

Handicappers who release picks early

Early lines are often soft lines; handicappers who release picks early often use these soft lines. They would not have gotten the soft lines had they released their picks closer to game time. At first glance this seems great for the handicapper's followers, as they get the opportunity to bet into a soft early line. But followers of handicappers who release picks early risk the chance that they will not find those lines. This is because sportsbooks are quicker to move early lines. If the handicapper has many followers, then it is easier for all of them to bet his plays if he releases on game day when all sportsbooks have lines at their normal limits. If the handicapper releases picks early, then some followers may miss plays due to line movement caused by other followers' bets.

Handicappers who have few followers do not have the same problem in releasing their plays early because the followers are not competing with too many other followers for the same lines. But once the handicapper gets more popular and signs up more clients, then followers as a group will suffer. This is a problem when considering a handicapper's record. If the handicapper did well in the past, the same records may not be duplicated by bettors in the future even if the handicapper's record stays constant.

Let's say there is a good basketball handicapper who releases picks the day before game day using overnight lines. He has picked winners at a 54% over a large number of picks, all using overnight lines. If you are able to find and bet the same lines as the handicapper used for his picks, then you should also expect to win at a 54% rate. On average, you have noticed that the lines move a half point on all his picks by the next morning. If you are not able to make bets in the overnight market and have to wait until the next day to make bets, then it is no longer worthwhile to follow this handicapper. A half-point move in basketball will drop a 54% win rate to about 52.2%. If you can bet into only lines with -110 juice, then there is no positive EV in betting the handicapper's picks at that rate. The handicapper is good and he is not trying to fool anyone. But at the same time, his picks are not useful to you since you cannot bet them.

Websites for Handicappers

There are pick-tracking websites that track wins and losses for picks of handicappers. These sites rank the handicappers in terms of their performances. Bettors who are looking for good handicappers often run into the problem of using a shotgun approach in looking at these lists. In picking out a handicapper to follow, it seems logical to look at a list of the top handicappers in a particular season in a particular sport. But this is dangerous. Here is an analogy using random coin flips.

Assume that there are 100 coin flippers, each flipping a coin 50 times, with heads counted as wins and tails counted as losses. If the coin flippers are ranked in terms of their win rate, a few of them will have phenomenal results due to the laws of probability. But since we know that they are coin flippers, we know the differences between their performances are random, and there are no good reasons to think they can control whether the future flips are heads or tails.

A bettor who looks at a list of 100 sports handicappers will look at the top few and think they are quality handicappers. The semi-sharp bettors will plug the handicappers' records into the binomial distribution formula shown earlier in this section and come up with impressive results. But they are falling into a possible trap, since the laws of probability say that even if all the handicappers' selections are random, a few handicappers will show great results. Following these handicappers may not make sense.

The experience of many bettors who follow handicappers is that rarely does a handicapper near the top of one of these season-long lists finish near the top again in a future season.

Other Relevant Information

Aside from the handicapper's record, there is other relevant information that you can gather to help you make a judgment on whether to bet a handicapper's picks.

Write-ups

A write-up is a description of the handicapper's reasons for making a pick. They can be useful or useless depending on the content and the handicapper. They can be useful if the write-up shows how the handicapper used logic, creativity and statistics in his reasoning for his pick. Write-ups are useless if they do not contain the reasoning for the pick.

Good write-ups include sound logic and/or statistics that justify the pick. If you are impressed by the write-up, you may be willing to follow the handicapper's play even without a large record of previous picks.

An illogical or bad write-up can be a sign that the handicapper is not as good as his record implies. Factual mistakes, erroneous assumptions and illogical statements are negative signs. Consistency in write-ups of different games between the same teams is important too. A handicapper's W-L record is just part of the story; it can be influenced by a lucky run.

Although write-ups can be useful, sometimes it is difficult for handicappers to pinpoint a specific reason why they picked a game. This is the case in particular for statistical handicappers. These handicappers feed their computers with relevant data and the computer spits out fair value lines based on the calculations programmed by the handicapper. It may be tough for the handicapper to separate one statistic from another; thus he will have a tough time pinpointing the exact reason why his system produces a line different from the bookmaker's line. For statistical handicappers, write-ups are not nearly as telling as they are for situational handicappers.

Size of other clients

The existence of big bettors (large bets, not fat bettors) following a particular handicapper is bad for the other followers. A client betting big has a higher chance of moving the line. It is worse when the big bettor bets quickly after a pick is released. Clients that are slower to bet the picks may not be able to find the same lines. If the handicapper's other clients are not big bettors, then you will have a higher chance of getting the same lines that the handicapper released. Unfortunately the better record a handicapper shows, the more followers he will probably have. With more people following any handicapper, it becomes more likely for any individual follower to miss a line. This paradox means followers may need to be on a continuous search for other good handicappers because the picks released by established handicappers may be tougher to find.

Change in pick volume

A handicapper whose pick volume changes during the season may be manipulating his full-season W-L record at your expense. His pick volume should not be based on his season-to-date W-L record. Be aware of this possibility and watch out for surprisingly high or low volume of picks.

A handicapper having a losing season may increase his pick volume in hopes of getting lucky and raising his W-L percentage. The more picks he makes, the higher his chance of getting even or ahead. These handicappers know that if they end the season with a losing record, they will have a tougher time attracting clients next season. So they try a "hail Mary pass" and make a lot of picks hoping to get lucky. If they get lucky, then their record will be better and their future outlook is brighter. If they do not get lucky, then their future outlook stays the same. A handicapper who called himself Yosh did just this a few years back, so some people on Internet forums use the term "Yoshing" to describe this practice.

A handicapper having a winning season may decrease his pick volume to lower the chance of his record turning sour. In this case, followers are not getting their money's worth, and the best interest of the handicapper no longer aligns with the best interest of his followers. For example, a record of 56-44 (56%) against the spread in football is good, but a few losses can turn it into a break-even or losing record against the juice. If the handicapper continues to pick winners at 56% or better for the rest of the season, his record is not going to look much more impressive to the layman than it does now. But a losing streak will change his record from impressive to ordinary. To the handicapper, the downside of continuing to make picks at a normal rate is greater than the upside. Some handicappers who are doing well in the current season will decrease the number of plays near the end of the season, which protects the W-L record but is not in the best interest of followers.

Adjusting the number of picks late in the season may not be meant to fool the followers. It is possible that some handicappers naturally find good bets in the latter parts of the season at a different rate than in the earlier parts of the season. If you are suspicious of a handicapper adjusting his number of picks due to his record, it may be useful to compare the number of picks the handicapper made late in the season in previous years. If the number of picks the handicapper is making late in the current season is similar to the number of picks he made in previous seasons, then it may be that he often sees more (or less) value late in the season.

Strategically releasing picks

Some handicappers wait as long as they can before releasing a pick. If the line moves so that the handicapper can get a better line (get more points if he is on the underdog or lay fewer points if he is on the favorite), then he can use the better line for his pick. If the line starts to move the other direction, the handicapper will quickly release his pick while a few sportsbooks have not yet moved the line. These handicappers will release their picks at all times of day depending on when lines look like they are poised to move. This practice has positives and negatives.

Here is an example of this practice that helps followers. The line on the Bucs-Jets game has stayed fairly constant all week:

> Bucs +3.5 -110
> Jets -3.5 -110

On Thursday, a couple of the major sportsbooks move their line to:

> Bucs +3.5 -120
> Jets -3.5 +100

The handicapper now releases his pick and takes the Bucs +3.5 -110. Although some sportsbooks have moved the line to the Bucs +3.5 -120, there are still sportsbooks that have the Bucs +3.5 -110. You have no problem finding that line and you bet it. In this case, you have potentially benefited from the handicapper waiting to release his pick. He may have liked the Bucs +3.5 -110 all week, but he was waiting to see if there was line movement in the other direction. If the line had moved the other way at some sports-books, then the handicapper can release his pick at the better line. For example, if the line moved to the Bucs +3.5 +100, then he would have released the Bucs +3.5 +100 and you would have been able to save a few cents in the vig. As it turns out, the line moved the other direction to the Bucs +3.5 -120. If you were still able to get Bucs +3.5 -110, then there was no harm done in waiting in this case.

On the other hand, releasing a pick as a line is moving can be a negative for followers. There may be a small window of time to make the bet at the line that the handicapper used for his pick before the line moves at all sportsbooks. If the line moved in all sportsbooks to the Bucs +3.5 -120 by the time you noticed the pick, then you would have missed the pick at the Bucs +3.5 -110.

By using this strategy, the handicapper has released his picks to his advantage. His record on this game will be the same whether he released early or late. But if the line had moved in the other direction, then his record could be better as he gets a better line. However, this is not necessarily the case with his followers. His followers may miss some of the bets that the handicapper releases due to the strategic timing of the handicapper's picks.

Some handicappers release their plays this way to maximize the apparent predictive value of their picks. The handicappers are not concerned whether their clients are able to bet the picks or not, but instead are more concerned with getting the picks counted into their records.

The handicappers who use this strategy successfully are sharp bettors since they have a good idea of how lines move. This is good for attentive followers. It is not good for followers who may miss the pick's release. Handicappers who announce the time that they will release their picks make it easier for followers who are not glued to sports betting all day.

Line movement

Line movement after a handicapper releases his picks can be used as a measure of the handicapper's sharpness. If a line moves so that the line the handicapper used is no longer available (but hopefully after bettors had the opportunity to make their bets), then that is a good sign about the handicapper's abilities. If a line moves so that a better line can be bet into after the handicapper released his picks, then that is a bad sign. Here is an example: A handicapper releases a pick at 1 PM: Pacers +5.5

Situation 1: the line moves to Pacers +3.5

Anyone who bet the Pacers +5.5 when the handicapper recommended is happy. If the each number in the NBA is expected to land 3.5% of the time, then that means the Pacers +5.5 should win 7% more often than the Pacers +3.5. If the follower bet the Pacers +5.5 but did not agree with it, he is happy because he can hedge and play the other side with a 2-point middle possibility. (The hedge itself may not be a positive-EV bet, but the combination of the bets has positive EV.)

Situation 2: the line moves to Pacers +7.5

Anyone who bet the Pacers +5.5 as the handicapper recommended is now sad. The bettor who bet the Pacers +5.5 right away as the pick was released has 7% less chance of winning than if he had waited and taken +7.5 at game time.

More Tips for Followers

Picks using rogue lines

Ignore a handicapper's bets against rogue lines, which are lines that differ markedly from the market line. If the handicapper is able to bet into incredible lines, but you are not able to find those lines, then the handicapper's picks will not enhance your bottom line.

Also ignore any pick that a handicapper tells you about only after the game has been played.

Records may be biased

There are record-keeping websites for handicapping services. These record-keeping websites document the winning percentages of handicapping services and allow people to view handicapper's past records without subscribing to the services. Professional touts are the main clients of these services. Even though the data seem transparent, people can be fooled by the information on these sites.

A poster on Internet forums by the handle of Joeflex has noticed that some record-keeping services allow handicappers to get the best line on some games even if those lines were not available. For example, the Warriors open as -1 against the Clippers, but the line moves to the Warriors -2 by game time. Handicappers who pick different sides are graded by different numbers. The record-keeping service may grade the handicapper who chose the Warriors with a line of -1, while grading the handicapper who chose the Clippers with a line of +2. If the handicappers made their picks at the right time (the former making the pick early and the latter making the pick late), then it is possible that this is a fair line to use for both handicappers. But too often, Joeflex has found, this is not the case, and in fact the record-keeping services are allowing handicappers the best lines of the day regardless of when the picks were actually made.

Record-keeping services can play other tricks that skew the results to the benefit of handicappers. This includes using lines from sportsbooks that deal dual lines (sharp lines for sharp players and square lines for square players; naturally the record-keeping service uses the square lines that are tough to find), and using rogue lines. Since record-keeping services are paid by the handicappers (directly or indirectly), their actions are not surprising.

Using break-even handicappers for cover

Betting the picks from break-even handicappers can be useful for cover purposes. A break-even handicapper against -110 lines is expected to win at a 52.4% rate. If you bet the picks of a handicapper expecting a 52.4% win rate, you have zero EV on your -110 bets. Such plays can be useful if you play a lot of proposition bets and few straight plays. Some sportsbooks discourage and/or kick out players who bet only on props. A prop player who also makes straight bets may be allowed to continue playing longer than one who bets only props.

Why does the handicapper sell picks?

Why does a handicapper sell picks? The suspicion is that if the handicapper is so good, then why isn't he betting his own picks? Actually, some handicappers who sell picks do bet their own picks. Even the handicappers who do not bet may have good reasons for just selling their picks. Here are some legitimate answers to the question "If the handicapper is so good, then why is he selling his picks?"

☐ He may be betting his own picks and selling them after he makes his bets in order to supplement his income

☐ He may be located in a place where sports betting is illegal and he cannot get to Las Vegas on a regular basis

☐ He may have a small bankroll and can make more money by selling his picks than he can by making small bets

☐ He may enjoy the handicapping process of analyzing games and teams more so than the grind of finding and making bets

☐ His ultimate goal in his handicapping service may be to meet people in order to arrange a business relationship.

☐ His handicapping service may generate greater income than he expects to make betting.

Conclusion

Truly skilled handicapping services do exist. But there are also many untalented handicappers who are making a buck by selling non-positive-EV picks. Some of these may be scam artists. Evaluating a handicapper is important if you are considering following his picks.

CHAPTER 22
SPORTS BETS
IN UNUSUAL
PLACES

Embedded Sports Bets

Some promotions run by non-casino companies contain embedded sports bets. The cost of the product combo is the sum of the embedded sports bet and the cost of the product itself. You can find the cost of the product for shopping comparisons by subtracting out the value of the embedded sports bet.

Generally the embedded sports bet has minimal value. For example, some NBA teams give free fast food for ticket stubs if the home team wins while scoring more than 100 points. Fans have fun near the end of the game even if the outcome is not in doubt. Fast food is inexpensive, but people like to get something they think is free (even if they theoretically paid for it).

Free Big Mac

Here is an example of valuing a free conditional giveaway in a NBA game. Let's assume the following:

> a ticket costs $50
> a Big Mac costs $3
> home team must win and score over 100 points
> the chance of that occurring is 25%

The value of the embedded sports bet can be calculated with the information listed above.

Value of embedded sports bet
    = Chance of sports bet winning x Value of prize
    = 25% x $3
    = $0.75

True cost of product (ticket to the game)
    = Cost of combo – Value of embedded sports bet
    = $50 - $0.75
    = $49.25

You paid $50, and you can consider that as $49.25 to watch the game and $0.75 for a bet on the home team to win while scoring more than 100 points at 3 to 1 odds.

On April 10, 2007, the Chicago Bulls had this exact promotion. If the Bulls won and scored 100 points or more, each fan would receive a Big Mac from McDonald's. The Bulls built a big lead early against the New York Knicks. At the end of the 3rd quarter, the score was 78-50. Near the end of the game the fans started getting excited about the Bulls passing the century mark. The Bulls played hard, trying to win a Big Mac for their fans. While ahead by more than 25 points in the last 1:04, they attempted and missed three three-point shots. Final score: Bulls 98, Knicks 69. Some Knicks players felt insulted that the Bulls were trying to run up the score. After the game a couple of Knicks yelled at the Bulls and there was almost a fracas. That was the final game of the season between those two teams. It will be interesting to see if this incident carries over to when the same teams meet for the first time in the 2007-08 season. Will the Knicks remember the Big Mac insult and play with more intensity? They say they will.

Embedded futures bet

Embedded sports bets can be futures bets as well, and can have high value.

Jordan's Furniture in Massachusetts and New Hampshire promised to refund the purchase price of any mattress, dining table, sofa or bed bought March 7 through April 16 of 2007 if the Red Sox win the 2007 World Series. My April 2007 estimate on the Red Sox winning the World Series was 12 to 1 or 7.7%. You can figure out the true cost of the furniture by subtracting the 7.7% value of the prize. Every $1,000 of purchase could be considered $77 of futures bet and $923 of furniture.

Furniture buyers are not usually interested in betting on sports. But whether or not they know it, betting on sports is exactly what Jordan's Furniture's customers were doing. They bought furniture at a 7.7% discount, and the discount came in the form of a bet. Jordan's Furniture's sales were fantastic during the promotion.

Jordan's Furniture announced it had insurance on the promotion, so it was not rooting against the hometown team. Thus the insurer of the promotion, rather than Jordan's Furniture, was the de facto sportsbook.

Options on Super Bowl Tickets

Ticketreserve.com is a website where you can purchase the right to pay face value for final-event tickets for particular teams. For example, you can buy tickets for a specified team to play in the Super Bowl. This is similar to options traded in the financial markets. You can sell only items that were originally purchased from Ticketreserve.com.

The options at Ticketreserve.com give you the right and obligation to purchase tickets at face value. Options in the financial markets are different in that the buyer has the right but not the obligation to buy. Demand for final-event tickets is so high that the market price is much higher than face value. Anyone who owns options on a Super-Bowl-bound team will definitely be happy to purchase tickets at face value. Options on teams that do not make it to the Super Bowl drop to zero value.

Consider a fan who paid $50 for the option to buy a ticket on the Chicago Bears to play in Super Bowl XLI (in 2007). During the season the fan could track the market of the option at

Ticketreserve.com. He could have sold his option to another fan on that website. After the Bears won the NFC championship game to advance to the Super Bowl, the fan was required to pay face value ($700 in Super Bowl XLI) for the ticket, bringing his total cost to $750. The street price for a Super Bowl XLI ticket was in excess of $2,000. The fan's choices were attend the game at the bargain price of $750, or sell the ticket for $2,000 or more. Meanwhile a fan who had bought an option to the New Orleans Saints, the team the Bears beat to get to the Super Bowl, saw the value of his option drop to zero.

Pricing of options

The valuation of the options depends on another variable that may be tough to value: the street price of the Super Bowl ticket. Components that make up the street price of a Super Bowl ticket are:

☐ The fan base of the team: Teams from big cities probably have fans with more buying power than teams from small cities.

☐ The other team in the game: Options are anchored to one specific team, but the street price may depend on the other team as well.

☐ The location of the game: Detroit is not as popular a destination as Miami or Pasadena.

☐ The economy: When the economy is good, people are more willing to spend on luxuries like going to the Super Bowl.

Assuming you have estimated the street value of a Super Bowl ticket, you can calculate the value of the option.

SV = Street value estimate of a ticket based on the specified team making the Super Bowl

SB% = Estimate of the probability that the team makes it to the Super Bowl

Net present value of ticket = SV x SB%

Option Value = Net present value of ticket - face value of ticket

Example

It is the night before the NFC championship game between the Chicago Bears and the New Orleans Saints. The mid-market money line on the game indicates the Bears have a 57% chance of winning and playing in the Super Bowl. After research, you expect the street value of a Super Bowl ticket if the Chicago Bears make it to be $2,500.

SV = $2,500
SB% = 57%
Options price
    = ($2,500 x 57%) - $700
    = $725

Given these estimates, the options on Super Bowl tickets if the Bears make it there should trade around $725.

Drawbacks

Ticketreserve.com calls itself a "fan-to-fan marketplace." While it is true that fans can transact with each other when one of them initially bought options sells to another fan, Ticketreserve.com makes the initial sale of every option; fans cannot sell short. Fans cannot take advantage of overpriced options unless they had previously bought the options.

Option prices on Ticketreserve.com appear to be higher than fair value. But it is conceivable that prices on some options may sometimes be fairly priced or even cheap.

Ticketreserve.com also takes a commission for each trade. Look at the rules in the website before making any decisions.

Season Tickets

A friend owns basketball season tickets at his alma mater. Because he owns the season tickets, he has the right to purchase all post-season games at face value, including tickets to the Final Four if his alma mater gets there. He no longer lives close enough to attend regular-season games. However, he loves to go to the Final Four, and tickets to the Final Four in the NCAA tournament are hard to get and sell at a premium. He views his purchase of season tickets as options on face-value purchase of post-season tickets. There is strong demand for tickets to regular-season games, and so he has no problem selling his tickets at face value, mostly to friends. This is similar to the options that one can buy at Ticketreserve.com. The difference is that in order to get the post-season options, my friend has to sell his regular-season tickets or absorb their cost. If he breaks even on the sales of his regular-season tickets, then the effective cost of the option on the Final Four tickets was zero.

Fantasy Sports

In fantasy sports, team owners use their projections of player performances to draft and trade players. Their evaluation techniques are similar to those used by sports bettors who bet on player proposition bets.

Fantasy sports leagues often involve money: an entry fee and a prize for the winner, making them a form of sports betting. The major sports leagues embrace fantasy sports leagues, while simultaneously lobbying Congress to strengthen laws against sports betting.

The US website Protrade.com offers fake-money trading on fantasy points for individual athletes. Some betting exchanges located outside the US offer similar products for real money from time to time.

CHAPTER 23
INTERNET AND MEDIA

Internet Forums

There are several Internet forums for sports bettors. These forums are great places to pick up information, ask questions and get interesting ideas from other sports bettors. Now and then I read a post and it spurs me to make a bet or look at something from a different angle. Here are some good and bad points about sports betting forums on the Internet.

Good things about Internet forums

- ☐ News on teams and players
- ☐ News on the gambling industry
- ☐ Tips on picking and betting games
- ☐ Angles for certain situations
- ☐ Some good advice about gambling situations
- ☐ See other people's mistakes
- ☐ See what other sharp bettors are betting and thinking about

Bad things about Internet forums

- ☐ Bad advice given by unknowledgeable people.
- ☐ Information designed to mislead
- ☐ Internet flame wars
- ☐ Advertisements cloaked as posts
- ☐ Non-sports issues

To get the most from sports-betting forums, ignore useless posts and threads and read only posts likely to be informative and of quality. Get to know which posters know what they are talking about, and read everything they write. If you get involved in posting, you may make new friends interested in sports betting, which otherwise can be a lonely activity as people try to keep their ideas to themselves. Having knowledgeable sports-betting friends that you trust and with whom you feel comfortable sharing and discussing ideas can be valuable.

Internet forums on sports betting

Here are some worthwhile websites, in alphabetical order:

- ☐ EOG.com
- ☐ LasVegasAdvisor.com
- ☐ MajorWager.com
- ☐ SharpSportsBetting.com
- ☐ TheRX.com
- ☐ TwoPlusTwo.com

The popularity of individual gambling forums goes up and down. One year all the quality posters seem to be at one forum, then the next year another forum takes over. By the time you are reading this, there may be new websites that have more dedicated and experienced posters sharing information.

Other Websites

There are great resources for sports bettors on the Internet. Here are some of them and their best features.

- ☐ Covers.com: contains articles and a large database of historical lines and results from many sports.
- ☐ Donbest.com: updates current lines and line movements.

☐ GJUpdate.com: updates current lines and line movements.

☐ GoldSheet.com: large database of historical lines and results from many sports.

☐ SBRlines.com: updates current offshore lines and line movements.

☐ TheLogicalApproach.com: large database of historical lines, results, and other statistics from many sports.

☐ Wagerline.com: tracks picks and records of handicappers; also has historical line information.

Media Coverage

The media are great sources of information for sports bettors. Analysts and insiders report on sports with information that you cannot get elsewhere. Keep up with the news by reading newspaper and magazine articles, listening to sports talk radio programs and watching dedicated sports shows on TV. Local radio and TV shows often have useful tidbits of information about the local teams that are not reported to the rest of the nation. There are so many sources that it is often difficult to filter out the small nuggets of information, especially when there are so many teams and media outlets. (This is another reason why it is helpful for inexperienced handicappers to focus on one sport at a time.)

Here are some analysts that I read or listen to carefully anytime they write or say something:

MLB: Peter Gammons, Tim Kurkjian, Rob Neyer, Nate Silver
NBA: John Hollinger
NFL: John Clayton, Peter King, Chris Mortensen

Be careful to not be misled by the media. Most media people are squares when it comes to sports betting.

The media guarantee a win!

People in the media are always trying to predict winners in games. Some of them are knowledgeable while others are not. But they all seem to make a common error: They speak in terms of absolutes. For example, some phrases I have heard are: "Texas has no chance against USC in the BCS," "New England will dominate and kill the Jaguars in the cold weather" and "the defenses are too good; there is no way this game will go over 35." The people making these statements are clearly not true gamblers. Texas was a 7 point underdog to USC. This translates to about a 25% chance of winning the game; 25% is not close to 0%.

People in the media consider themselves to be in the entertainment business. They need good ratings just as much as the actors and actresses in other TV shows. So they need to be emphatic and controversial when picking who will win the game, even if doing so makes them sound like idiot gamblers.

Sharp gamblers will not typically speak or write in absolutes. They know that when they have an edge, it is usually small. Sharp gamblers are head and shoulders above the media when it comes to understanding odds and percentages.

Personal relationships with players

Sports reporters generally put too much emphasis on their personal relationships with players. They allow these personal relationships to influence them in their reporting as well as in voting for awards such as the MVP. The stories about the bad relationships two Red Sox players had with the Boston media are legendary. Both Ted Williams and Jim Rice had problems with the media and it hurt them in getting MVP votes (in Williams' case) and Hall-of-Fame votes (in Rice's case).

Here is an example of a current player and reporter. David Wright is one of the best players in baseball. Midway through the 2006 season he was a possible MVP candidate, but a weak one due to incredible seasons by Ryan Howard and Albert Pujols. Some reporters discussing Wright mentioned how nice a person he is. What does being nice to the media have to do with his MVP candidacy? Sports reporters get swayed by people they like, and are eager to write good things about the good guys. They are more willing to write bad things about players who do not treat them nicely. That is human nature. Their bias may also be present in their writing and commentary, consciously or subconsciously.

The media overrate NFL quarterbacks

The media often cite playoff records for NFL quarterbacks. Before the 2006 NFL playoffs, they constantly told us about Peyton Manning's 3-6 record in the playoffs and Tom Brady's 10-1 record. Those are true facts, but those facts can be misleading. When the media dish out those statistics, they are implying the respective records are due to the quarterbacks only. Brady gets all the credit for having a great playoff record, while Manning gets blamed for the Colts' poor playoff record. Why do quarterbacks get so much credit or blame? This is silly hype from the media and their focus on individuals rather than teams. The quarterback is the most recognized individual in football. Why don't the media tell us about Richard Seymour's record in the playoffs? As an important member of the Patriots defense, he played in every game that Brady did, so his record is the same. What about Orlando Pace's playoff record and the time that he allows his quarterbacks to throw the ball? What about Marvin Harrison? He played in all those playoff games that Manning did. His receiving record in the playoffs is subpar compared to his record in the regular season. Shouldn't he shoulder some of the blame too? More than any other sport, football is a team game. Focusing on just one player and giving him all the credit and all the blame is wrong. Too often that is how the media do their analyses of the NFL.

The media try to explain everything

Randomness is a word that does not seem to exist in the media's vocabulary. The media often try to explain the result of a game with a specific reason, such as one team "wanting to win" more than the other, a key coaching decision or an off-the-field issue. But often teams win or lose games simply due to randomness. There does not have to be a specific reason why the game turned out the way it did. If a basketball game is tied with 10 seconds to go, and there is a loose ball on the floor, the team that recovers the ball is not necessarily the team that wants to win the most. A player may coincidentally be in the exact spot he needs to be when a ball comes loose. Another player may have been in the perfect spot for a play to win the game, but the ball just went in different direction.

An example is the 1982 NCAA championship basketball game between Georgetown and North Carolina. Trailing by a point with eight seconds to go, Georgetown had the ball. While close to midcourt, Georgetown guard Fred Brown threw a pass to his right, directly to North Carolina forward James Worthy, who was out of position. Worthy has admitted that he made a bad defensive play by jumping out and leaving his man uncovered. He admitted it was complete luck that the ball was thrown to him. Neither team necessarily played harder or wanted to win more; the deciding play was due to randomness. But the media perpetuate the fictions that Worthy made a great defensive play to anticipate the pass and that North Carolina wanted to win more.

Gossip

Off-field gossip on star athletes is often sensationalized by the media. Celebrity gossip sells newspapers, magazines, and it increases television ratings. Gossip concerning star athletes in the past few years include: Tiger Woods' impending parenthood, Brian Urlacher dating Paris Hilton, Derek Jeter involved with Mariah Carey, Michael Strahan's bitter divorce proceedings and Michael Jordan's gambling losses

It may be fun to listen and read about the personal lives of athletes, but does any of this news impact their performance on the field? Data on this angle are tough to gather, but my thought is that the influence is negligible.

If star athletes falter, the media will sometimes connect problems in their personal lives to their failure on the field. But when a star athlete is having personal problems and continues to perform like a star, the media do not consider personal problems a factor, or they reason the athlete was able to draw strength from his problems and play with "heart." The media like to have an explanation for everything, and sometimes turn personal stories into causation stories after the game. If Tiger Woods does not win a tournament, they speculate that his marriage and impending parenthood were the reasons. On the other hand, when Brian Urlacher plays a great game after partying with Paris Hilton, there is no mention of the possible distraction. When Michael Jordan hit yet another game-winning shot, the media had amnesia about his gambling losses. Had he missed the shot or played an unexpectedly bad game, some media members undoubtedly would link his poor play to his gambling losses.

The moral is to understand the media's agenda. Do not be fooled when they are fooled or when they are trying to relate performance on the field to an off-field incident. You do better at sports betting if you don't allow the media's opinions on off-field issues to influence you.

CHAPTER 24
INTERVIEW
WITH A PRO

In Las Vegas there are professional bettors who act in groups similar to trading groups in the financial markets. I met some members of a large group and was impressed with their operation. They would fit in perfectly in the pits of the futures exchanges. I contacted a member of the group and asked if he was willing to give an interview for my book; he agreed. He posts on some Internet forums under the handle "the Chaperone."

Q: Which sports did your group bet and why did you choose those sports?

A: We primarily bet football and basketball. The main reason is they are the most popular sports and thus provide opportunities for a group like ours to get down large volume without moving the market so far that the value disappears. The popularity of the sports also helps provide opportunities with rogue numbers. For example, it's not uncommon for a high-rolling table-games player to bet 50K on his alma mater. Most books probably don't really want this action, but they don't want to upset their favorite baccarat player; so they take it. Then they move the line, begging groups like ours to come in and bet the other side large. If the line moves far enough, we oblige. You just don't see this kind of thing often with NHL or MLB.

Of course there are also times when you catch the book sleeping and bet a stale number large. The bigger the sport, the less they mind, as our large bet is just a drop in the bucket compared to their entire NFL handle. You tend to get a different attitude when you bet a stale Arena Football total.

Don't get me wrong though. We would bet anything if we felt there was an edge (or just a scalp or middle opportunity). We've bet on boxing, UFC, NHL, MLB, women's basketball, etc. Baseball is always tempting. The limits are low, but there are so many betting opportunities. Unfortunately, to this point my group is not convinced that we have much of an edge betting bases. It doesn't help that most of us had no interest being in Las Vegas during the summer.

Q: What were your responsibilities in the group?

A: For two years I was a runner, and the third year I was the primary shot caller (the person who makes the major decisions and remains in the office in communication with the runners).

A lot of people look down on runners saying things like 'any monkey could be a runner.' Well, any monkey could be a mediocre runner. There are guys who are paid to sit in one book all day and bet when they are called upon. My group was much more dynamic and the runners were much more involved in group operations. First of all, everyone was invested in the group and received a percentage of the results, win or lose. Secondly, we never sat around in one place. It was not uncommon for one runner to bet at 10 different sportsbooks in a day, and many of them more than once. I was a great runner and I took pride in that. Right now there are probably two or three guys running in Vegas that are as good as I was, maybe ten more who are fairly good and then of course there are a bunch of monkeys.

You may ask what makes for a good runner. Well, it mostly comes down to hustle, smarts, and experience. As far as hustle is concerned, it could be running a red light, driving down the emergency lane for a couple blocks, or just plain running to the window or running from book to book. Not everyone is physically capable or willing to bet at Caesars, the Mirage and the Venetian during the same halftime!

Being intelligent helps because if you understand what is going on and why you are betting something, you are less likely to make mistakes. You also may spot something that perhaps your shot caller missed. (He is busy after all!) Perhaps you see a 1st half or money line that looks a little better than the game point spread you are betting. Maybe call the shot caller and check. Maybe you run to the window to bet a game before kickoff, but the line has moved from -4.5 -110 to -5 -105. A sharp runner knows to bet -5 -105. In this situation, most runners will call their shot caller to check on the bet; but stepping out of the sportsbook to make a phone call takes time, and they risk the game kicking off and missing the bet.

Experience comes into play mostly when navigating the streets and parking garages of Las Vegas. Knowing the best roads and places to park is important as it saves quite a bit of time over the course of a season. If you can't figure out how to get from the Las Vegas Hilton to the Palms in ten minutes, you lose. (Hint: Desert Inn and Valley View.) It also helps to know who the competing runners are. I've seen a guy waiting at the Wynn elevator, oblivious as I blew by him and ran down the stairs and beat him to the number. I've also seen a runner walking into a book while I'm looking for parking. That's what the handicapped spots are for. Park there and run by him to the window. It's a dog eat dog world!

Being the shot caller was far less interesting. It was mostly just looking at line services, using proprietary software, gathering picks from our favorite touts, updating spreadsheets and exposures, and lots of time on the phone. I spent thousands of minutes every month on the phone, along with hundreds of text messages. Thank God for Verizon's IN Calling plan!

Q: How did the group handle differences in ideas? What if people in the group had differing opinions on a bet?

A: We had a general strategy for betting tout picks and rogue numbers going into the season. We really didn't have many differences of opinion on what was a good bet. There was more of an issue with bet sizing. We all agreed on a particular Kelly fraction, though in order to determine the proper wager with the Kelly Criterion, you need to have a good idea of how much your advantage is. It's virtually impossible to compute your precise advantage with sports betting, so disagreements could arise. It was mostly the job of the shot caller to make a final decision, but he would often consult other senior members of the group. There were certain cases where we ended up vastly overexposed on a particular wager. For example, getting down on Dr. Bob's (a well known tout) plays in the 2006 football season was a pain. We would have as many as 10 guys trying to wager either in Las Vegas or on the Internet. Sometimes none of us would get the bet in. Other times all of us would. When we all did, we could end up with 80k on a game when we really wanted only 40k. Senior members of the group would have a mini-conference in these situations. Sometimes we would bet back at reduced vig. We had the advantage that the market generally moved in our favor on those plays (sometimes it was our own doing!); and we could often scalp or get out of a position for free.

Q: How many hours per day or per week were you working? How much of that time was spent driving and/or walking from one sportsbook to another?

A: As a runner, I probably worked 60 hours a week during football season, and 40 hours a week during basketball season with virtually no days off. Needless to say, November is a pain. At least half of that time is in transit. I almost never just sat around in a sportsbook.

As the shot caller, it was probably more like 80 hours a week. The only advantage of being the shot caller is that you don't have to drive in that traffic and you don't have to cash the tickets. There's nothing worse than having to go out into Saturday night Las Vegas traffic to cash tickets to get money to bet on rogue NFL numbers in the morning.

Q: How did you communicate with the rest of the group? Was there ever a chance two or more people in the group would make the same wager and you guys would double-up by accident?

A: We communicated primarily by cell phone, text messaging, and conference calls. Occasionally we used email if we had someone in Reno or something, but that was rare. Of course we'd double up by accident on occasion. In this case we were actually helped by the low limits of Vegas books. It's not that big a deal if you end up with $20,300 on a game when you were shooting for $20,000; every now and then Harrah's takes a bet when you don't expect it.

This was a problem only a few times and it generally had to do with a mad rush to get down on ridiculously out of whack favorite money lines before the kickoff of big games.

Q: When were the majority of your football bets made? Before game day or on game day?

A: Mostly before game day. We'd bet some rogue numbers Saturday and Sunday morning, and we also bet halftimes. But we generally had the positions we wanted before game day.

Q: Was it more difficult to get bets down on game day?

A: Not really. A lot of books have windows that catered to high limit bets only. Since we were betting large amounts, we generally qualified. Even though a lot of books didn't like us picking off their bad numbers on Wednesday, most of them were more than happy to take our action on NFL Sunday.

Q: How much did you guys deviate into the relative-value or derivative type of plays, such as first halves, quarters, props and futures?

A: Not enough! This is one thing that I started getting into towards the end of my year as the shot caller. There's not a lot of quarter betting in Vegas, but definitely there is value in first halves and money lines, not to mention some correlated unmentionables. Our group generally didn't bother with futures as we felt it was more important to roll our money over every week getting a 2-3% return weekly, rather than getting a bigger advantage while tying up our money for a number of weeks or months with a futures bet. Props are few and far between in Vegas. There's definitely value at some of the online shops. You would probably want a prop expert to really focus on them. We generally didn't bet them much outside of the Super Bowl.

Q: Were you ever kicked out of a sportsbook for winning too much or being too sharp?

A: Absolutely. This trend was ushered in by Harrah's and Caesars Palace in 2005, and has caught on at some of the Vegas books. There's virtually no book in Vegas that has never kicked out a sharp. They generally fall into three categories:

1. Sportsbooks that bar straight bettors.
2. Sportsbooks that deal dual lines. When you try to bet a number on the board, the book moves the line a half point against you.

3.   All the other books will back you off of parlay cards or other exotics if you are pounding them too hard. You can usually go back the next week. But maybe not if you hit a few 10-team parlays!

Q: What was the sportsbooks' rationale for kicking you out? Were they simply scared of your action?

A: Who knows? They usually don't give you a reason. Chasing steam is the thing that brings the most heat. I assume it's because they want to sit there, drink their coffee and read the paper rather than staying on top of the market. I mean how hard is it to watch the Don Best screen? Yes, they are obviously scared of my action. A lot of times, it's probably just jealousy. Somehow I don't think 40-year-old guys who work for the man like 20-somethings like me coming into their book every day splashing around a lot of cash and profiting from their mistakes or laziness.

Q: I understand you also play blackjack. Did the sportsbooks ever make the connection between your sports betting and blackjack counting? Did your blackjack play increase the chances of sportsbooks booting you?

A: I have no way of knowing for sure, but I don't think so. The general rule in casinos is that the right hand doesn't know what the left hand is doing. Why else do I keep getting comped to suites at Caesars? I've been backed off from blackjack three times, including one attempted trespass. I can't bet sports at any of its associated properties. But I still get free rooms, tournament invites, and travel cash.

Well, I don't think it's any different with sports and table games. I think there have been one or two cases where my heavy sports action has provided cover at the blackjack tables. Big blackjack action, big sports action, throw in a little video poker and you look like a well-rounded sucker. There have been cases where I've been chased off the property following a blackjack session and returned a few days later to bet large on football with no problems.

GLOSSARY

10-cent line: a line in an event where the two opposing bets are 10 cents apart. For example, if the favorite is -110 and the underdog is +100, the game has a 10-cent line.

Accompanying money line: the money line that is attached to a point spread, also called the juice, the vigorish and the vig.

Angle: a idea used as a reason for a category of picks.

Betting lines: the prices that the sportsbook put up for customers to wager on. All betting options are included.

Board: the sportsbook posts its lines on its walls.

Book: sportsbook.

Buying points: bettors get more points in exchange for paying more juice. Half-point buys often cost 10 additional cents in basketball and football (modify the accompanying money line of the point spread to get the new juice with the extra half point by adding ten cents for favorites and subtracting ten cents for dogs), but it may cost more on certain key numbers.

Cents: a measurement of differences in money lines. See chapter 3 for more details.

Chasing steam: betting a side that is poised to move due to other people betting the same side; usually associated with a popular handicapper releasing a pick.

Cost-basis: the price you pay to purchase a ticket.

Cover (n): a bet or activity that may help prevent you from being identified as a sharp bettor by a sportsbook.

Cover (v): to cover a point spread means to win the wager.

Data-miner: a person who looks for patterns or trends in a database of results without regard for the logical reasoning behind them.

Dime bet: a $1,000 bet. When a customer comes up to the betting window and wants to bet $5,000, the teller may turn to the supervisor and say: "the customer wants five dimes on this game."

Dime line: same as a 10-cent line. A line which has a total vig of 10 cents, for example: favorite -120, underdog +110.

Dog: same as underdog.

Early line: betting lines that are put up by the sportsbook well before the game. In football, it is as much as a week before the game. In sports with daily games, it is usually the day before the game (overnight lines).

Edge: same as positive EV.

Efficient line: a line that accurately portrays the true odds in the sporting event

Exact series line: lines on whether or not a certain team will win the series in a specific number of games.

Expected Utility (EU): a mathematical term describing the average result of happiness over the realm of all outcomes.

Expected Value (EV): a mathematical term describing the mean result of values over the realm of all outcomes.

Expiration of futures: when the event of the futures play actually occurs. A Super Bowl future's expiration is the Super Bowl.

Fading lines: sportsbooks adjusting their lines due to action or in anticipation of action

Fair market line: see market line.

Favorite: the side expected to win the game or event.

Follower: a bettor who bets other handicappers' picks.

Fundamental handicapping: handicapping by looking at the qualities of the teams and players through statistical analysis and other objective measures.

Futures: wagers whose outcomes will be decided after a long time period, such as a full season of play.

Game day: the day of the event.

Game of the year lines: lines for future games that are usually the most anticipated games of the year. These lines are commonly put up for big football games.

Game time: immediately before the game starts.

Give points: see lay points.

Get points: an underdog get points in the point spread by adding the points to the underdog's game score.

Handicapper: a person who evaluates games or events and tries to pick winners against betting lines.

Hedge: a bet that reduces the risk in another bet.

Juice: see vigorish.

Lay points: a favorite lays points in the point spread line by subtracting the points from the favorite's game score.

Margin of victory (MOV) betting line: a betting line on a specific range of points between the two teams. For example: the Colts to win by 14 to 20 points pays 4 to 1.

Margin of victory (MOV) statistic: a statistic that measures the average point difference between a team and its past opponents. A negative MOV means a team has been outscored.

Market line (fair market line, mid-market line): the line that is in the middle between the best lines from different sportsbooks. If the best money line on Team A is -150 and the best money line on Team B is +146, then the market line is Team A -148, Team B +148.

Mid-market line: see market line.

Middle: a game score that lands between different betting lines.

Middling: betting on each of two opposing teams. There must be a game score that would win both bets.

Money line: the line used to represent how much you have to lay to win 100 or how much you win when laying 100. -150 means you lay 150 to win 100. +150 means you risk 100 to win 150.

Moving on action: when a sportsbook moves a line due to betting action.

Moving on air: when a sportsbook moves a line due to seeing other sportsbooks moving their lines.

Negative-EV bet: a bet on which an average outcome would be a loss.

Nickel bet: a $500 bet. See dime bet for a similar example.

Nickel line: same as a 5-cent line. A line which has a total vig of 5 cents, for example: favorite -120, underdog +115.

Opportunity costs: the cost of missing a chance to make a positive-EV investment due to funds being tied up in another investment.

Overnight lines: lines that are put up the night before a game for sports with games on a daily basis, such as baseball, basketball and hockey.

Parlay: a bet involving two or more teams where all teams must win in order for the bet to win.

Parlay (Correlated): a parlay in which the picks are related to each other such that if one wins, then the other is more likely to win than previously thought.

Point spread: a betting line that adds points to the game score of the underdog and subtracts points from the game score of the favorite.

Point spread, Alternate: a second and different point spread than the regular point spread. The accompanying money line on the alternate point spread is usually not close to even money as it is for regular point spreads. For example, when the regular point spread is -3.5 -110, an alternate point spread may be -7.5 +190.

Positive EV: see Expected Value.

Positive-EV bet: a bet that wins on average. If you make such bets repeatedly, you expect to make money in the long run.

Proposition bets (Props): a bet on other than who will win or how many points will be scored by both team combined. Props can be on individual player statistics, team statistics, the timing of certain events in the game, and many other issues. Props on the Super Bowl are popular.

Push: a bet that is refunded with no winner or loser when the outcome is a tie or when there is no defined winner or loser.

Regular season wins: an over/under bet on the number of wins by a team during the regular season.

Relative-value plays: a bet that is made by comparing the value of one wager to another.

Releasing picks: when handicappers communicate their picks to their followers.

Reverse middle: the position that loses in a middle when a game score that lands between different betting lines.

Rogue line: a line that is different from the line at most sportsbooks.

ROI: return on investment, a term that measures the rate of profit over total investment. See chapter 2 for more details.

Run line: a baseball betting line in which one team lays 1.5 runs and the other gets 1.5 runs.

Runner: a member of a betting group who takes instruction from a shot caller and makes the bets in sportsbooks.

Scalp: two bets that oppose each other but are made at different prices to capture a profit with zero risk.

Semi-sharp player: a player that knows a few things about sharp play but does not know enough to adjust when times change.

Settlement of futures: see Expiration of futures.

Sharp bettor, sharp player: a bettor who understands the betting markets and often makes positive-EV wagers.

Shot caller: the member of a betting group who makes important decisions and relays information to runners.

Soft lines: betting lines that are relatively easy for sharp players to beat.

Sportsbook: the entity that takes sports bets from customers.

Square bettor, square player: a bettor who does not understand the betting markets well and often makes predictable negative-EV wagers.

Stale line: a line that has not changed at one sportsbook but has at most others.

Strength of schedule: the quality of a team's opponents.

Team, as in two-team parlay: A parlay consists of multiple picks. The picks do not have to be teams in the sense of Redskins and Packers. The "teams" in a parlay can be sides, totals, player props, first halves, and any other betting line a sportsbook allows you to use in a parlay.

Teaser: a parlay with additional points added to each team. All teams must cover the modified spreads for the teaser to win.

Tilt: losing self-control. Often means overbetting or making a bet that you would not have made when thinking rationally.

Time value of money: the value of future money adjusted for interest rates.

Total: a betting line that you use to bet the over or the under.

Tout: a handicapper who sells picks. Often this term is used in a derogatory manner. Handicapper is a more neutral, non-derogatory term.

Trend: sequential events that seem to have something in common.

Underdog: a player or team that is not expected to win the event.

Vigorish, Vig: the amount of edge the sportsbook builds into the betting line.

Widely available lines: a level in a line that is easy for most bettors to find and bet. If more than a third of sportsbooks have the line at that level, then it can be said to be widely available.

Zero-sum game: an activity where what one party wins exactly matches what another party loses.

Zigzag theory: a theory that postulates the team that lost the previous game in a playoff series has a better chance of covering the spread in the next game.

INDEX

BOOKS BY PI YEE PRESS

Bryce Carlson's *Blackjack for Blood* discusses counting cards at blackjack. It contains an excellent level 2 counting system.

Tino Gambino's *The Mad Professor's Crapshooting Bible* discusses beating craps. Its strengths are discussions of grips, tosses, practice tips, adjusting to table conditions, dice setting, and betting.

Bob Nersesian's *Beat the Players* describes how the rights of casino customers are abused by casinos and law enforcement. Nersesian is a lawyer who has won many lawsuits brought by customers, particularly advantage players, against casinos.

Stanford Wong's *Wong on Dice* discusses beating craps. It covers rules, sets, gripping, and tossing. Its strengths are practice tips and advice on dice setting and betting.

Stanford Wong's *Casino Tournament Strategy* explains how to get an edge over the other players in casino-games tournaments. It covers blackjack, craps, baccarat, keno, and horses.

Stanford Wong's *Professional Blackjack* has a complete and accurate presentation of the *high-low*, the counting system used by more card counters than any other because of its combination of simplicity and power. If you want a more advanced counting system, *Professional Blackjack* also contains the *halves*.

Stanford Wong's *Blackjack Secrets* explains how to get away with playing a winning game of blackjack in casinos. It also contains an introduction to the high-low card counting system.

Stanford Wong's *Basic Blackjack* is a comprehensive presentation of basic strategy and win rates for all common rules and most exotic rules for the game of blackjack. It also explains methods of getting an edge that do not involve counting cards.

Stanford Wong's *Sharp Sports Betting* explains how to bet sports, primarily NFL football. It covers home field advantage, the trade-off between the money line and betting against the spread, totals, teasers, money management, betting sports on the Internet, props on season win totals, and use of the Poisson distribution to analyze other props.

Stanford Wong's *Optimal Strategy for Pai Gow Poker* shows how to get an edge at pai gow poker, and includes advice on setting every possible hand.

King Yao's *Weighing the Odds in Hold'Em Poker* discusses limit hold'em. Topics include sizing up your opponents, counting "outs," figuring pot odds, the value of position, determining when to raise, call, or fold, bluffing, semi-bluffing, slowplaying, check-raising, regular games, shorthanded games, and playing poker on the Internet.

King Yao's *Weighing the Odds in Sports Betting* discusses sports betting. Topics include betting NFL, NBA, MLB, triple crown horse races, college basketball, season wins, Super Bowl props, scalping, middling, hedging, and more.

Ordering Information

The easiest way to order is to use the online order forms on www.SharpSportsBetting.com and www.BJ21.com. Or you can visit in person or write to Pi Yee Press, 4855 West Nevso Drive, Las Vegas NV 89103-3787. Or email orders@SharpSportsBetting.com. Or call 702-579-7711.